The Tradition Continues at IMHS

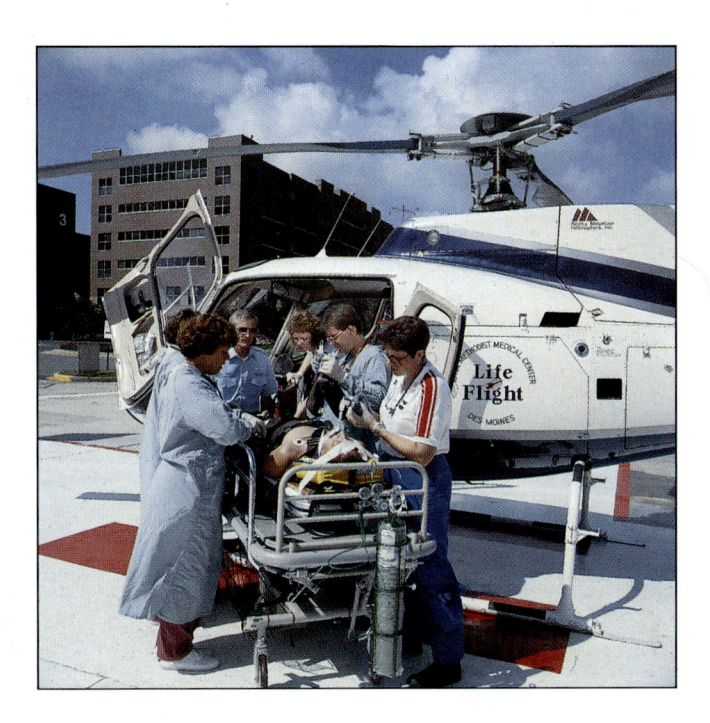

LIFE FLIGHT

As central Iowa's only designated trauma center, Iowa Methodist offers the services of a trauma surgeon in-house, 24 hours a day. Iowa Methodist became the first hospital in central Iowa to offer air ambulance services in 1979 with the inception of Life Flight. The helicopter transports more than 800 patients each year.

The Tradition Continues at IMHS

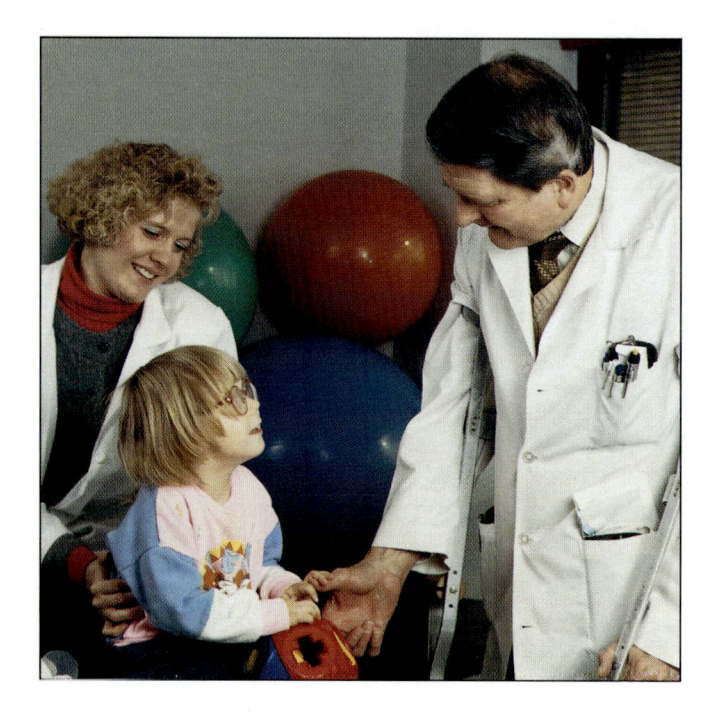

DR. DE GRAVELLES WITH CHILD PATIENT

Younker Rehabilitation Center has been treating patients for more than 30 years and is nationally recognized for its range and quality of services. Superior rehabilitative care in services including physical, occupational and speech therapy offer maximum independence to individuals with severe disabilities.

Contents

Acknowledgements	4
Introduction	5
Nourishing Volunteers	6
Contributor List	7
The Tradition Continues	13
Appetizers and Beverages	19
Soups and Sandwiches	27
Salads	39
Meat and Meatless Main Dishes	55
Poultry and Seafood Main Dishes	75
Vegetables and Side Dishes	91
Breads	103
Desserts, Candy and Cookies	115
Cakes and Pies	135
Charts	148
Nutritional Guidelines	157
Index	158
Order Information	163

ACKNOWLEDGEMENTS

Iowa Methodist Health Foundation wishes to recognize and thank those volunteers who have assisted in compiling the recipes in the cookbook "Iowa Methodist Banquet."

Group Affiliate Contacts

Mike Rodemyer—Administration/Medical Staff
Ann Kenworthy—Boards of Directors
Suzanne Dostal—Employees/Employee Activity Committee
Pat Veler—Employees/Employee Activity Committee
Paula Thornton—Iowa Methodist Nurse Alumni
Helen Westfall—Raymond Blank Hospital Guild
Marge Lawlor—SixtyPlus
Cindy Ashby—Younker Rehabilitation Alumni

Thank you to all who took the time to care by sharing their favorite recipes with us.

We acknowledge the invaluable assistance provided by Iowa Methodist Public Relations and Food and Nutrition departments. We also wish to recognize the Board of Directors of Iowa Methodist Health Foundation for adoption and promotion of the cookbook project.

Caring. Our patients at Iowa Methodist are central to everything we do. We pledge excellence to all those who depend on us.

INTRODUCTION

Some of the best times experienced in any community are times spent around the table. Sharing food, be it a banquet or snack, builds bonds, strengthens ties and nourishes in many ways.

The community now called Iowa Methodist Health System is far too large for its many thousands of members to sit around a single table, but it is in the spirit of this community and its bonds that this cookbook is created.

The creation and contributions to the cookbook involved many groups and hundreds of individuals with coordination by the Iowa Methodist Health Foundation. Many have contributed to the menu.

Ultimately, thousands will share this "Methodist Banquet" through their purchase of these recipes. All funds received above the costs of the cookbook (approximately 50%) will go to maintain and enhance the caring and healing provided to Iowa Methodist patients.

Sharing. Sharing fun times build bonds at Iowa Methodist.

Nourishing Volunteers

The rich tradition of the "Volunteer" continues at Iowa Methodist. From the early days when Iowa Methodist was started with a gift through the days when eggs, jams and jellies from the farm fed Iowa Methodist patients—the generosity of individuals formed the basis of excellence on which Iowa Methodist stands.

That tradition of volunteering continues to play a critically important part in today's healthcare delivery.

Voluntary support groups which serve Iowa Methodist patients on a day-to-day basis and who have been important in the development of this cookbook include members of the Boards of Directors, Medical Staff and spouses, Iowa Methodist employees, Iowa Methodist School of Nursing Alumni, Raymond Blank Hospital Guild, Powell CDC Association, Younker Rehabilitation Alumni Association and on and on and on.

Photographs and messages throughout this book point out the centers of excellence of Iowa Methodist Health System.

Adult Volunteer with Baby. The Raymond Blank Hospital Guild, with more than 1,000 members, offers innumerable services to Iowa Methodist Medical Center. A strong force of 700 adult and teen volunteers donate more than 65,000 hours each year to help maintain the caring quality at Iowa Methodist Medical Center.

Contributor List

Glenda Ahrenstorff
Lucille Anderson
Sandra Arnold
Cindy Ashby
Janet Bailey
Laura Baker
Connie Beasley
Margaret K. Beatty
Stephanie Becker
Mary Belknap
Miriam E. Bennett
Nondas Beswick
Glennys Bittick
Chris Blair
Margaret Blair
Donna R. Blochowitz
Kathy Brandenberg
Jessie Bohner
Nancy and Norm Bone
Marian Brenton
Dorothea Brown
Kay Bucksbaum
Mary Lou Burns
Camille Calhoun
Marjorie Canine
Ruth Carey
Jane C. Chamberlain
Marie Champlin
Mary Clarke
Louise Clifton
Shelley Clifton
Gloria Gilchrest-Cole
Margaret Coffman
Mrs. Don Cordes
Barb Cotter
Natalie Creighton
Joanne Cutler
Rose Marie Dachenbach
Marci Drannen
Sheila Drevyanko
Sandy Donohoe
Betty Doolittle

Steve Dunap
Cynthia Eby
Patricia L. Edwards
Kay Elliott (Steve)
Betty L. Erickson
Hazel Evans
Suzanne Farrington
Sharon Fettig
Dee Fowler
Deb Fry
John Gay
Mrs. Maurice Gibbons
Lynn Gossen
Lois Grisamore
Mrs. Chas. Gutenkauf
Joel E. Hade
Deborah Herzberg
Virginia A. Hill
Roxanne Hircock
Dorothy Hoeness
Nancy Jo Hopkins
Beverly Hoyle
Darwin Hucka
Jean Hulse
Vicki Huyser-Eatwell
Lois Ives
Linda Jackson
Paul Jackson
Belva Jaquis
Jane Jinkinson
Rachael C. Johnson
Ruth Jones
Margie Kautzky
Joyce Keen
Karen Kehoe
Nola Kimpton
Louise King
Melissa Kirk
Betty V. Knapp
Edna Lange
Kate Benson Larson
Marge Lawlor

June Lovejoy
Margaret B. Lowe
Ivan W. Lyddon
Sheila Malone
Dorothy C. Mann
Marjorie S. Marks
Heyoung McBride
Marjorie McBride
Debbie McCloney
Karen McGregor
Lorraine Meehan
Elaine Mefford
Dorothy A. Middlekoop
Debra Montufar
Bev Morris
Robin L. Morse
Pat Mower
Zoe E. Nichols
Marie Nicoll
Alice Nielsen
Joan Nielsen
Christine M. Nims
Eleanor Noel
Shawn Nugent
Pat Overton
Jerry Paul
Rhonda Paul
Betty S. Perry
Mary Peterson
Adina Phillips
Sara Meyer Phillips
Toni Pickard
Euletta Popp
Betty Raife
Elinor Ramsey
J. Joan Rebec
Janna Rensch
Steve and Sue Reynolds
Elaine S. Rex
Margaret Riccio
Charlene W. Roach
Carol Rogers

James D. Ryken
Callie Sandquist
Joann Sargent
Phyllis L. Scheib
Charlotte Schlenker
Barbara Schmitt
Judy Schneller
Eloise Schultz
Don Ireland-Schunicht
Susan Smith
Jane Spieker
Martha Squire
Sheri Stainbrook
Jewel Storlie
Alvin Storlie
Mildred F. Studer
Kamy Sullivan
Margaret Swanson
Helen Ticknor
Lisa Turner
Barbara Tuttle
Dorothy Tuttle
Doris Ullestad
Ruth Van Note
Fran Venter
Iola Washburn
Minerva Weber
Pat Weber
Marjorie L. Weider
Jo Wertman
Rebecca Westberg
Helen Westfall
Sharon Williams
Lou Ann Willis
Deanna Wilson
Renee Winans
Randy Winston
Dianne Wood
Dixie Hagge Wyatt
Mildred A. Yarrow
Jan Yoder
Delores L. Young

The Tradition Continues at IMHS

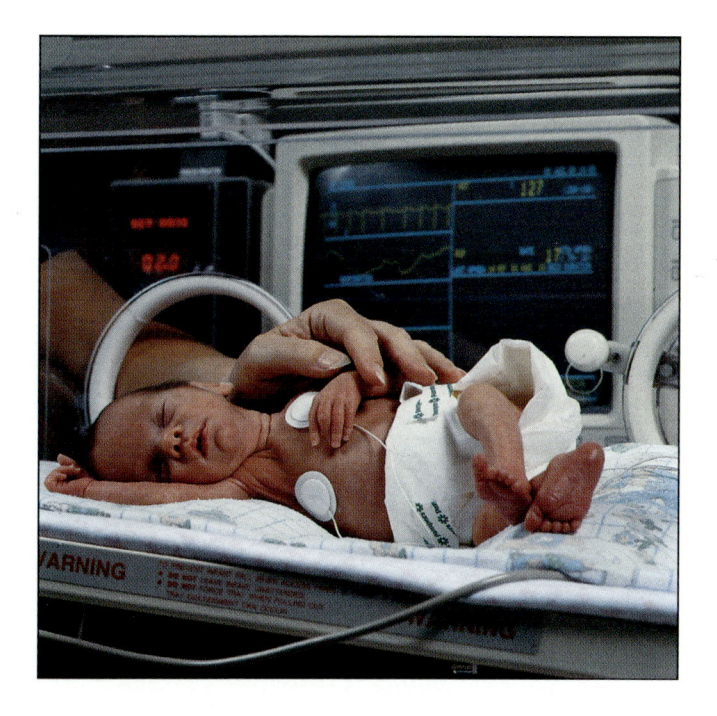

Raymond Blank Children's Hospital

Iowa Methodist is the home of Raymond Blank Memorial Hospital for Children, the only free-standing children's hospital in Iowa. The Variety Club Neonatal Intensive Care Nursery is designated as a Level III nursery and provides the highest level of care of pre-term and critically ill newborns.

The Tradition Continues at IMHS

ONCOLOGY NURSE WITH CHILD PATIENT

At Iowa Methodist, cancer treatment is available on both an inpatient and outpatient basis. The John Stoddard Cancer Center offers the most advanced diagnostic and therapeutic treatments for patients, currently ranking in the top one percent nationally in terms of new cancer cases diagnosed and/or treated. Blank Children's Hospital is home to the Variety Club Children's Cancer Center, a member of the Children's Cancer Study Group which includes other major cancer treatment centers in the United States.

1940s Polio Shot. During the severe poliomyelitis epidemic which began in 1949, the Raymond Blank Memorial Hospital for Children became the center for care of stricken patients. The disease was so highly contagious that even parents were not permitted to visit their children.

90 years have passed since IMH opened its doors.

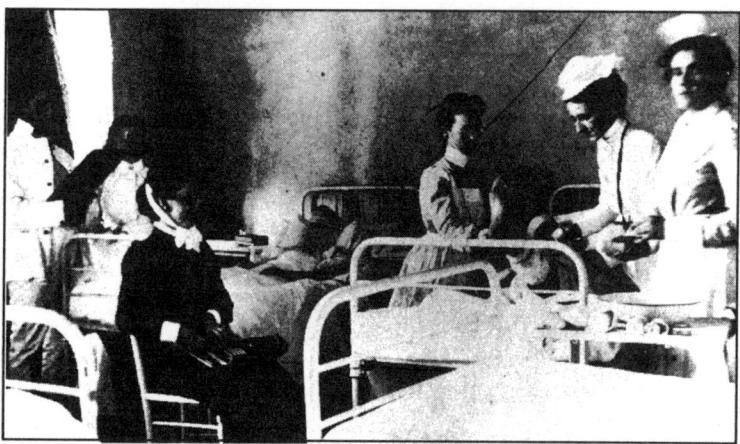

1900s Hospital Scene. More than 90 years have passed since Iowa Methodist Hospital opened its doors to the people of Des Moines. What started as a small 30-bed hospital is now one of the region's largest health care systems. Iowa Methodist Health System includes Iowa Methodist Health Foundation; Regional Health Services, Inc. and Iowa Methodist Medical Center all working together to promote the availability of quality, cost effective healthcare services throughout the region.

Advanced Technology. Cutting edge technology and a caring philosophy touch patients at Iowa Methodist.

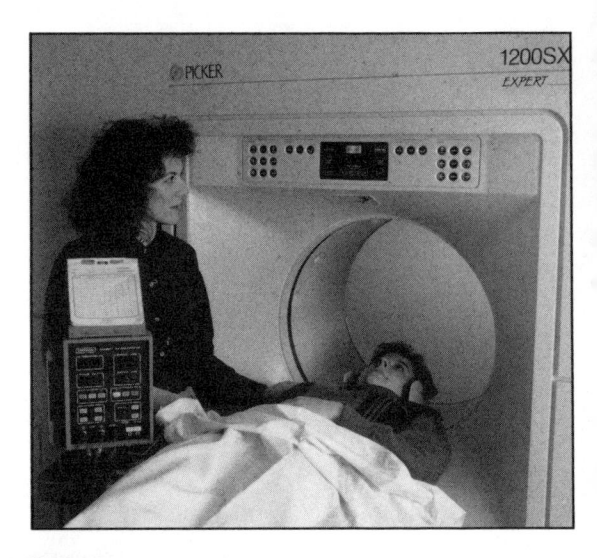

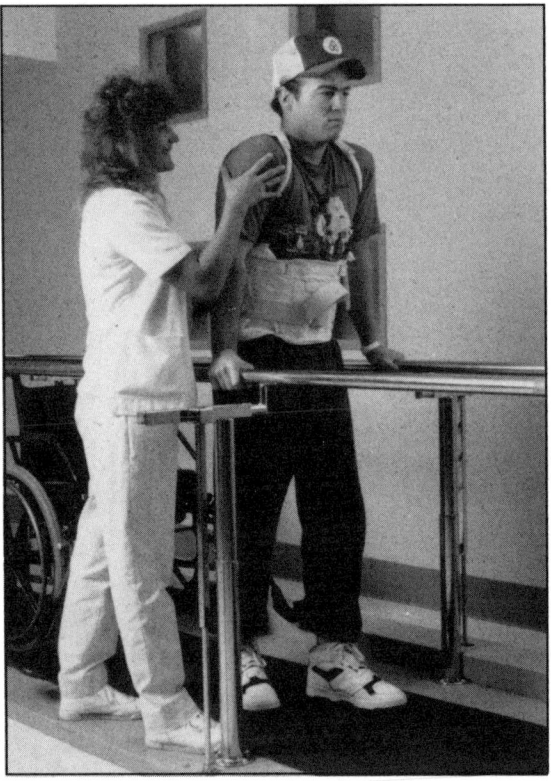

Physical Therapy. The Younker Rehabilitation Center exemplifies a comprehensive team approach to treatment that provides the necessary foundation for patients to achieve productive and purposeful lives. More than 18,000 patients have been treated at Younker in its 30 year history.

Younker Rehabilitation Center is nationally recognized for its range and quality of service.

The Blank Playroom. Medical staff and patients enjoy time spent in the playroom.

*R*aymond Blank Children's Hospital provides the highest level of care for Iowa's children.

Playing. Children and parents have an opportunity to relax and have some fun in the Blank Children's Playroom.

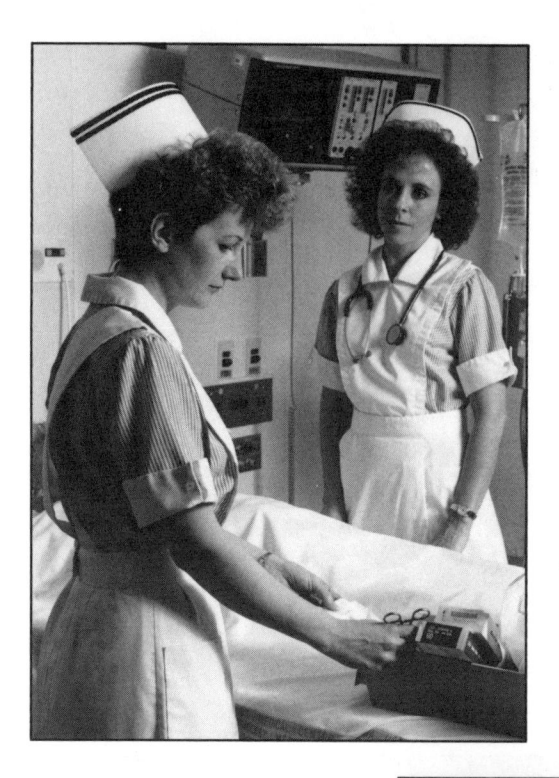

Learning. Student nurses acquire confidence and skill in bringing their technical knowledge to their work with patients.

*I*owa Methodist's commitment to excellence in the future of healthcare is evident in the many educational opportunities at the Medical Center.

School of Nursing. The Iowa Methodist commitment to excellence in the future of healthcare is evident in the many educational opportunities available at the Medical Center. Educational programs include: School of Nursing; Residencies in Internal Medicine, Pediatrics and Surgery, Radiologic Technology; Clinical Lab Scientist Program and Clinical Pastoral Education; Chemical Dependency Counsellor Training; Administrative Fellowships and Continuing Education for physicians, nurses and other specialities.

FOT. Since 1984 the Des Moines **Festival of Trees** volunteers have worked to provide funds for the children in need at Raymond Blank Children's Hospital. Fun, food and festivities abound at this annual Thanksgiving week community event.

The Iowa Methodist pledge of excellence continues in its volunteer efforts and medical outreach program.

Perinatal Van. Iowa Methodist reaches out to hundreds of communities throughout Iowa and beyond through home care, educational programs and consulting services.

Cardiac Patient. From angioplasty procedures to complete coronary bypass, Cardiovascular Services patients are cared for by cardiac professionals utilizing the latest equipment in the most up-to-date facilities.

Gerontology. Iowa Methodist's Gerontology Department serves the healthcare needs of older Iowans. With the SixtyPlus program, members can take advantage of a variety of services including seminars and free health screenings.

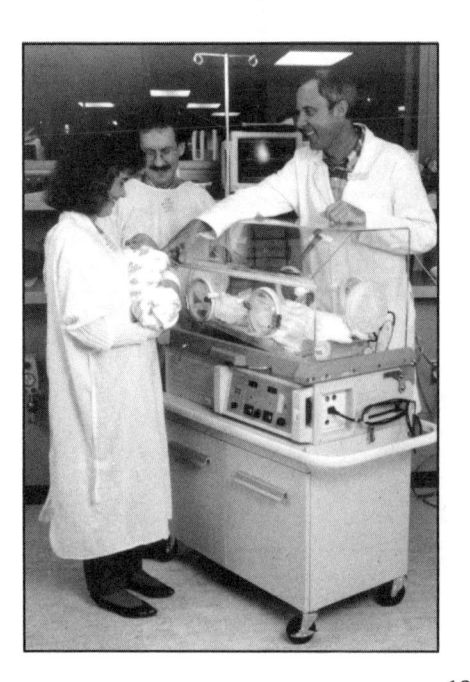

Nursery Family. While the bricks and mortar may have changed, one thing that has remained constant throughout the years is Iowa Methodist's commitment to quality patient care.

Iowa Methodist is committed to quality patient care.

Appetizers and Beverages

CHEESE CHILI SQUARES

Yield: 36 servings   Utensil: baking pan   Preheat: 350 degrees

8 eggs
½ cup flour
1 teaspoon baking powder
¾ teaspoon salt
1½ cups cottage cheese
3 cups shredded Monterey Jack cheese
2 4-ounce cans green chilies, chopped

Beat eggs in large bowl. Add flour, baking powder and salt; mix well. Fold in cottage cheese, Monterey Jack cheese and chilies. Pour mixture into greased 9x9-inch baking pan. Bake at 350 degrees for 40 minutes. Cool for 10 minutes. Cut into squares.

Approx Per Serving: Cal 71; Prot 5 g; Carbo 2 g; Fiber <1 g; T Fat 5 g; Chol 57 mg; Sod 155 mg.

CRABMEAT CANAPÉS

Yield: 16 servings   Utensil: baking sheet   Preheat: 400 degrees

1 5-ounce jar Old English cheese spread
½ cup butter, softened
½ teaspoon seasoned salt
¼ teaspoon garlic powder
1 tablespoon mayonnaise
1 6-ounce can crabmeat, drained, flaked
6 English muffins

Beat cheese and butter together in bowl until smooth. Add seasoned salt, garlic powder, mayonnaise and crabmeat; mix well. Split muffins; cut into quarters. Spread with crabmeat mixture. Arrange on nonstick baking sheet. Bake at 400 degrees for 10 minutes or until golden brown. Serve hot. May be frozen before baking and stored in freezer. Bake frozen as needed.

Approx Per Serving: Cal 155; Prot 6 g; Carbo 11 g; Fiber 1 g; T Fat 10 g; Chol 32 mg; Sod 423 mg.

STUFFED MUSHROOMS

Yield: 12 servings　　Utensil: baking pan　　Preheat: 350 degrees

1 pound fresh mushrooms
1 6-ounce can tuna, drained
¼ cup finely chopped celery
¼ cup finely chopped green onions
¼ cup mayonnaise
½ cup cracker crumbs
4 ounces Parmesan cheese, grated

Wash mushrooms; remove stems. Combine tuna, celery, green onions, mayonnaise and cracker crumbs in bowl; mix well. Stir in half the cheese. Stuff mushrooms with mixture. Arrange in 9x13-inch baking pan. Sprinkle with remaining cheese. Bake at 350 degrees for 10 to 15 minutes or until cheese is melted. Serve immediately. May also bake in microwave. May substitute crabmeat for tuna.

Approx Per Serving: Cal 130; Prot 9 g; Carbo 7 g; Fiber 1 g; T Fat 7 g; Chol 20 mg; Sod 334 mg.

SPINACH-STUFFED MUSHROOMS

Yield: 20 servings　　Utensil: baking pan　　Preheat: 400 degrees

1 12-ounce package frozen spinach soufflé, thawed
⅓ cup herb-seasoned bread crumbs
⅓ cup grated Parmesan cheese
½ teaspoon lemon juice
Dash of hot pepper sauce
20 large fresh mushrooms
2 tablespoons melted butter

Combine spinach soufflé, bread crumbs, Parmesan cheese, lemon juice and hot pepper sauce in large bowl; mix well. Rinse mushrooms; remove stems. Dip mushroom caps in melted butter. Arrange stem side up in 9x13-inch baking dish. Spoon 1 heaping tablespoon of spinach mixture on each mushroom; drizzle with remaining melted butter. Bake at 400 degrees for 15 to 20 minutes or until filling is puffed. Arrange on serving dish; serve hot.

Approx Per Serving: Cal 55; Prot 3 g; Carbo 2 g; Fiber 1 g; T Fat 4 g; Chol 27 mg; Sod 143 mg.

New Potato Appetizers

Yield: 24 servings   Utensil: saucepan   Preheat: no

1/2 cup sour cream
2 tablespoons chopped chives
24 small new potatoes
4 slices bacon, crisp-fried, crumbled

Mix sour cream and chives together in small bowl; set aside. Cook potatoes in boiling water in saucepan until tender; drain. Let stand until cool enough to handle easily. Cut in half; scoop out center with teaspoon or melon baller. Fill with sour cream mixture; sprinkle with bacon. Chill in refrigerator until serving time. May add 1/3 teaspoon garlic powder to sour cream mixture.

Approx Per Serving: Cal 90; Prot 2 g; Carbo 17 g; Fiber 2 g; T Fat 2 g; Chol 3 mg; Sod 25 mg.

Sausage Puffs

Yield: 8 servings   Utensil: baking sheet   Preheat: 350 degrees

1 12-ounce package mild pork sausage
1 12-ounce package hot pork sausage
4 ounces Swiss cheese, shredded
1 tablespoon grated Parmesan cheese
1 tablespoon dried parsley
1 teaspoon basil
1 teaspoon garlic powder
Salt and pepper to taste
3 eggs
1 18-ounce package frozen puff pastry, thawed
1/2 cup Dijon mustard
2 tablespoons honey

Brown sausage in heavy skillet until crumbly; drain. Combine cooked sausage, Swiss and Parmesan cheeses, parsley, basil, garlic powder, salt and pepper to taste in large bowl; mix well. Beat eggs in bowl. Reserve 2 tablespoons beaten eggs for glaze. Stir remaining eggs into sausage mixture. Roll 1 sheet of pastry into 12x17-inch rectangle. Place half of the sausage mixture on one side of rectangle. Fold over, pinching ends to seal tightly. Repeat with remaining sheet of pastry and remaining sausage mixture. Arrange in semi-circle on nonstick baking sheet. Bake at 350 degrees for 30 to 40 minutes or until golden brown. Cool for 10 minutes; cut into 1 1/2-inch thick slices. Combine mustard and honey in small bowl; mix well. Serve with sausage puffs. May use egg substitute in place of eggs.

Approx Per Serving: Cal 540; Prot 17 g; Carbo 36 g; Fiber 1 g; T Fat 36 g; Chol 135 mg; Sod 1036 mg.

Fluffy Fruit Dip

Yield: 20 servings	Utensil: blender	Preheat: no

8 ounces processed cheese, cubed
1 16-ounce can cream of coconut
8 ounces whipped topping
Red food coloring

Combine cheese and cream of coconut in blender container. Blend at high speed until mixture is smooth. Spoon into bowl. Fold in whipped topping. Tint pink with food coloring. Chill in refrigerator until serving time. Serve with fresh assorted fruits.

Approx Per Serving: Cal 144; Prot 3 g; Carbo 5 g; Fiber <1 g; T Fat 13 g; Chol 6 mg; Sod 156 mg.

Taco Dip

Yield: 8 servings	Utensil: serving plate	Preheat: no

3 avocados, peeled
1 tablespoon lemon or lime juice
1 cup sour cream
1 envelope taco seasoning mix
2 8-ounce cans refried beans
1/2 cup chopped tomatoes
1/4 cup chopped black olives
1/4 cup chopped green onions

Mash avocados with lemon juice in small bowl until smooth. Mix sour cream with taco seasoning mix in bowl. Layer refried beans, avocado mixture, sour cream mixture, tomatoes, olives and green onions on serving dish. Serve with tortilla chips.

Approx Per Serving: Cal 260; Prot 6 g; Carbo 19 g; Fiber 13 g; T Fat 20 g; Chol 13 mg; Sod 319 mg.

Dip for Strawberries

Yield: 6 servings	Utensil: mixer bowl	Preheat: no

1 cup marshmallow cream
1 tablespoon lemon juice
1 tablespoon orange juice
1/4 cup mayonnaise

Combine marshmallow cream with lemon juice and orange juice in mixer bowl; whip until fluffy. Fold in mayonnaise. Spoon mixture into serving dish. Chill in refrigerator until serving time. Serve with strawberries.

Approx Per Serving: Cal 208; Prot 1 g; Carbo 37 g; Fiber <1 g; T Fat 7 g; Chol 5 mg; Sod 78 mg.

Hot Crabmeat Spread

Yield: 10 servings Utensil: baking dish Preheat: 375 degrees

8 ounces cream cheese, softened
1 tablespoon milk
1 7-ounce can crabmeat, drained, flaked
½ teaspoon horseradish
2 tablespoons finely chopped onion
¼ teaspoon salt
¼ teaspoon pepper
⅓ cup sliced almonds, toasted

Beat cream cheese and milk in small bowl until smooth. Add crabmeat, horseradish, onion, salt and pepper; mix well. Spoon into 5x9-inch baking dish. Sprinkle with toasted almonds. Bake at 375 degrees for 15 minutes. Serve warm with crackers.

Approx Per Serving: Cal 118; Prot 6 g; Carbo 1 g; Fiber <1 g; T Fat 10 g; Chol 43 mg; Sod 188 mg.

Party Spread

Yield: 20 servings Utensil: springform pan Preheat: 350 degrees

16 ounces cream cheese, softened
2 cups shredded Cheddar cheese
1 cup sour cream
1 envelope taco seasoning mix
3 eggs
1 4-ounce can chopped green chilies, drained
⅔ cup salsa
1 cup sour cream
1 avocado, peeled, chopped
2 or 3 hot red peppers, chopped
Fresh parsley

Combine cream cheese and Cheddar cheese in mixer bowl; beat well. Add 1 cup sour cream and taco mix; mix well. Add eggs 1 at a time, beating well after each addition. Fold in chilies. Spoon mixture into 9-inch springform pan. Place on baking sheet. Bake at 350 degrees for 35 to 40 minutes or until center is almost set. Cool for 10 minutes. Combine salsa with remaining 1 cup sour cream; mix well. Spread over cheese mixture. Bake for 5 minutes longer; cool. Chill in pan for 3 hours to overnight. Remove to serving dish. Garnish with avocado, peppers and parsley. Serve with chips.

Approx Per Serving: Cal 215; Prot 7 g; Carbo 5 g; Fiber 1 g; T Fat 19 g; Chol 79 mg; Sod 343 mg.

LIVER PÂTÉ

Yield: 10 servings　　Utensil: blender　　Preheat: no

3/4 pound chicken livers
3/4 cup butter, softened
3 tablespoons minced onion
1/2 teaspoon nutmeg
1 teaspoon dry mustard
1/8 teaspoon ground cloves
Dash of cayenne pepper
Salt to taste

Place chicken livers in enough salted water to cover in saucepan. Cook, covered, for 10 minutes. Drain, reserving 1/4 cup liquid. Cut chicken livers into small pieces; place in blender container. Add butter, onion, nutmeg, mustard, cloves, cayenne pepper and reserved 1/4 cup liquid. Blend at high speed until mixture is smooth. Stir in salt to taste. Spoon mixture into serving bowl. Chill for 30 minutes before serving. Serve with crackers.

Approx Per Serving: Cal 162; Prot 6 g; Carbo <1 g; Fiber 0 g; T Fat 15 g; Chol 197 mg; Sod 129 mg.

HOLIDAY PUNCH

Yield: 60 servings　　Utensil: punch bowl　　Preheat: no

2 envelopes unsweetened cherry drink mix
1 envelope unsweetened orange drink mix
1 envelope unsweetened raspberry drink mix
4 1/2 cups sugar
4 quarts water
1 16-ounce can frozen orange juice concentrate, thawed
1/2 gallon raspberry sherbet, softened
2 quarts ginger ale

Combine cherry, orange and raspberry drink mixes with sugar in bowl. Stir in water and orange juice concentrate until blended. Chill in refrigerator until serving time. Pour mixture into large punch bowl. Add raspberry sherbet. Pour in ginger ale; stir gently.

Approx Per Serving: Cal 117; Prot <1 g; Carbo 29 g; Fiber <1 g; T Fat 1 g; Chol 2 mg; Sod 15 mg.
　　Nutritional information does not include drink mixes.

Wedding Punch

Yield: 80 servings   Utensil: punch bowl   Preheat: no

2 6-ounce cans frozen lemonade concentrate
1 6-ounce can frozen orange juice concentrate
9 cups water
5 pints pineapple sherbet
1 quart vanilla ice cream

Thaw concentrates. Combine with water in large pitcher, stirring until blended. Chill until serving time. Soften sherbet and ice cream slightly. Place in punch bowl. Pour orange juice mixture over sherbet and ice cream, stirring slightly.

Approx Per Serving: Cal 58; Prot 1 g; Carbo 12 g; Fiber <1 g; T Fat 1 g; Chol 5 mg; Sod 17 mg.

Orange Julius

Yield: 6 servings   Utensil: blender   Preheat: no

1 6-ounce can frozen orange juice concentrate, thawed
1 cup milk
1 cup water
1/2 cup sugar
1 teaspoon vanilla extract
10 to 12 ice cubes

Combine orange juice concentrate, milk, water, sugar, vanilla and ice cubes in blender container. Blend on high speed until mixture is smooth. Serve in tall, chilled glasses.

Approx Per Serving: Cal 146; Prot 14 g; Carbo 32 g; Fiber 0 g; T Fat 8 g; Chol 34 mg; Sod 22 mg.

Hot 'n' Spicy Punch

Yield: 30 servings   Utensil: saucepan   Preheat: no

1 cup red-hot candies
4 cups water
4 3-ounce packages strawberry gelatin
3 quarts apple cider
1 gallon cranberry juice cocktail

Combine red-hot candies and water in saucepan. Bring to a boil, stirring frequently until candies are dissolved. Add gelatin; stir until dissolved. Add cider and cranberry juice cocktail. Heat until mixture is bubbly, stirring constantly. Serve hot.

Approx Per Serving: Cal 180; Prot 1 g; Carbo 45 g; Fiber 1 g; T Fat <1 g; Chol 0 mg; Sod 42 mg.

Soups
and
Sandwiches

Borsch

Yield: 4 servings Utensil: food processor Preheat: no

1 15-ounce can beets
¼ cup sugar
Juice of 1 lemon
1 teaspoon salt
¼ cup egg substitute
1 beet can water
¼ cup plain yogurt

Drain beets, reserving juice. Combine half the beets with reserved liquid in food processor container. Process with steel blade for a few seconds until smooth. Pour into bowl. Grate remaining beets with grating disc. Add to beet mixture. Stir in sugar, lemon juice, salt, egg substitute and water; mix well. Chill for 4 hours. Serve in individual chilled bowls with a dollop of yogurt.

Approx Per Serving: Cal 107; Prot 4 g; Carbo 22 g; Fiber 2 g; T Fat 1 g; Chol 1 mg; Sod 989 mg.

Cucumber-Yogurt Soup

Yield: 4 servings Utensil: blender Preheat: no

1 cucumber, peeled, seeded, chopped
1 cup water
¼ cup minced onion
¼ cup chicken broth
1 tablespoon flour
¾ cup chicken broth
1 bay leaf
1 cup non-fat yogurt
Juice of ½ lemon
1 fresh mint leaf, minced
2 tablespoons coarsely chopped walnuts

Combine cucumber, water and onion in saucepan. Bring to a boil. Pour ½ of the mixture into blender container. Process until smooth. Blend ¼ cup chicken broth with 1 tablespoon flour in small bowl. Combine with remaining ¾ cup chicken broth in saucepan. Simmer for 2 minutes; remove from heat. Stir in cucumber mixture, bay leaf, yogurt, lemon juice, mint leaf and walnuts. Chill for 2 hours. Remove bay leaf before serving.

Approx Per Serving: Cal 95; Prot 6 g; Carbo 11 g; Fiber 1 g; T Fat 4 g; Chol 4 mg; Sod 236 mg.

Gazpacho

Yield: 12 servings　　Utensil: food processor　　Preheat: no

½ cucumber, thickly sliced
1 onion, thickly sliced
1 large green bell pepper, seeded, sliced
8 tomatoes, cut into wedges
5 cloves of garlic
1 cup tomato juice
¼ cup olive oil
¾ teaspoon chili powder

Combine cucumber, onion, green pepper and 7 tomatoes in food processor container. Process until coarsely chopped. Pour into large bowl. Combine remaining tomato, garlic, tomato juice, oil and chili powder in food processor container. Process at high speed until ingredients are blended. Add to vegetable mixture; mix well. Chill before serving. May store for up to one week in refrigerator.

Approx Per Serving: Cal 69; Prot 1 g; Carbo 7 g; Fiber 2 g; T Fat 5 g; Chol 0 mg; Sod 81 mg.

Artichoke Shrimp Soup

Yield: 4 servings　　Utensil: saucepan　　Preheat: no

1 16-ounce can artichokes, drained, chopped
1 6-ounce can small shrimp, drained
1 4-ounce can mushroom pieces, drained
1 10-ounce can cream of celery soup
2 soup cans milk
½ teaspoon curry powder
½ teaspoon pepper

Combine chopped artichokes, shrimp, mushrooms, soup and milk in saucepan; mix well. Stir in curry powder and pepper. Simmer gently for 30 minutes, stirring frequently. Pour into soup tureen; serve hot.

Approx Per Serving: Cal 256; Prot 19 g; Carbo 26 g; Fiber 1 g; T Fat 10 g; Chol 103 mg; Sod 907 mg.

BEST-EVER SOUP

Yield: 10 servings   Utensil: saucepan   Preheat: no

1½ pounds ground beef
5 cups water
3 beef bouillon cubes
4 carrots, sliced
4 green onions, thinly sliced
⅓ cup barley
¼ cup catsup
1 28-ounce can tomatoes, chopped
1 8-ounce can tomato sauce
8 ounces fresh mushrooms, sliced
2 bay leaves
Salt and pepper to taste
1 10-ounce package frozen green beans
10 tablespoons shredded Cheddar cheese

Brown ground beef in skillet, stirring until crumbly; drain. Bring water to a boil in large saucepan. Add bouillon cubes, stirring to dissolve. Add carrots, green onions, barley, catsup, tomatoes, tomato sauce, mushrooms, bay leaves, salt and pepper; mix well. Simmer for 1½ hours, stirring occasionally. Add green beans. Simmer for 30 minutes longer. Remove bay leaves. Serve in individual bowls garnished with shredded Cheddar cheese. Make one day ahead for best flavor; skim before reheating.

Approx Per Serving: Cal 261; Prot 19 g; Carbo 20 g; Fiber 5 g; T Fat 13 g; Chol 52 mg; Sod 722 mg.

SOUR CREAM-BROCCOLI SOUP

Yield: 6 servings   Utensil: blender   Preheat: no

½ bunch fresh broccoli
½ head cauliflower
1 medium onion
1 cup chicken broth
1 teaspoon nutmeg
1 cup sour cream
1 10-ounce can cream of mushroom soup
2 tablespoons butter, softened

Cut broccoli, cauliflower and onion into bite-sized pieces. Combine with chicken broth and nutmeg in saucepan. Cook over medium heat for 6 minutes or until vegetables are tender-crisp. Pour into blender container. Add sour cream, cream of mushroom soup and butter. Blend at high speed for 20 seconds. Pour into saucepan. Heat until warmed through, stirring frequently.

Approx Per Serving: Cal 200; Prot 5 g; Carbo 11 g; Fiber 2 g; T Fat 16 g; Chol 28 mg; Sod 606 mg.

Cheese Soup

Yield: 8 servings Utensil: saucepan Preheat: no

1 chicken bouillon cube
1 cup water
3 cups cubed potatoes
½ cup chopped celery
½ cup chopped carrots
¼ cup chopped onion
1 teaspoon parsley flakes
Salt and pepper to taste
1½ cups milk
2 tablespoons flour
8 ounces process cheese, cubed

Place bouillon cube in hot water in large saucepan, stirring until dissolved. Add potatoes, celery, carrots, onion, parsley, salt and pepper; mix well. Simmer, covered, for 15 to 20 minutes, stirring frequently. Blend milk and flour in small bowl. Stir into vegetables. Simmer until thickened, stirring constantly; remove from heat. Add cheese, stirring until melted. Pour into serving dish; serve warm.

Approx Per Serving: Cal 231; Prot 10 g; Carbo 25 g; Fiber 2 g; T Fat 11 g; Chol 33 mg; Sod 584 mg.

Cheesy Chicken Corn Chowder

Yield: 6 servings Utensil: saucepan Preheat: no

2 whole chicken breasts
½ cup chopped onion
½ cup celery
2 carrots, chopped
1 cup water
1 10-ounce can cream of chicken soup
1 10-ounce can chicken noodle soup
1 cup whole kernel corn
1 cup milk
1 cup shredded American cheese
2 tablespoons chopped pimento

Rinse chicken and pat dry. Combine chicken breasts, onion, celery, carrots and water in large saucepan. Bring just to the boiling point. Simmer, covered, for 15 to 20 minutes. Remove chicken breasts; cool until easily handled. Remove chicken from bones; chop chicken. Combine with soups, corn, milk, cheese and pimento in saucepan; mix well. Simmer for 10 minutes. Pour into soup tureen; serve hot. May also add chopped carrots.

Approx Per Serving: Cal 280; Prot 23 g; Carbo 20 g; Fiber 2 g; T Fat 12 g; Chol 63 mg; Sod 1233 mg.

EGGDROP SOUP

Yield: 2 servings | Utensil: saucepan | Preheat: no

2 14-ounce cans chicken broth
½ cup diced water chestnuts
1 tablespoon cornstarch
2½ tablespoons water
¼ cup chopped green onions
1 egg, slightly beaten

Add chicken broth to saucepan. Bring to a boil, stirring frequently. Add water chestnuts. Mix cornstarch with water in bowl, stirring until blended. Stir gradually into soup mixture. Add green onions. Cook until slightly thickened, stirring constantly. Remove from heat. Pour in egg slowly, stirring gently. Serve in individual bowls while hot.

Approx Per Serving: Cal 138; Prot 12 g; Carbo 10 g; Fiber 1 g; T Fat 5 g; Chol 108 mg; Sod 1300 mg.

GARBANZO SOUP

Yield: 12 servings | Utensil: soup pot | Preheat: no

1 pound bacon, cut into pieces
1 onion, chopped
2 16-ounce cans garbanzo beans, drained or 1 package dried chickpeas
1 16-ounce can tomatoes
6 to 8 potatoes, cubed
1 green bell pepper, chopped
2 cups cubed ham
1 teaspoon oregano
1 teaspoon basil
1 teaspoon parsley
¾ tablespoon chili powder
2 to 3 bay leaves
Salt and pepper to taste

Brown bacon and onion in skillet until bacon is crisp; drain. Combine with garbanzo beans, tomatoes, potatoes, green pepper and ham in 8-quart soup pot; mix well. Stir in oregano, basil, parsley, chili powder, bay leaves, salt and pepper. Simmer for 4 to 5 hours or until beans and potatoes are tender. Remove bay leaves before serving.

Approx Per Serving: Cal 386; Prot 20 g; Carbo 58 g; Fiber 9 g; T Fat 9 g; Chol 22 mg; Sod 568 mg.

HAM HOCK HEAVEN

| Yield: 6 servings | Utensil: saucepan | Preheat: no |

16 ounces dried lima beans
1 large potato, cubed
6 ham hocks
2 slices bacon
1 green bell pepper, chopped
1 onion, chopped
1 tablespoon light brown sugar
1/2 teaspoon Cajun seasoning
1 10-ounce can tomato soup

Soak lima beans in water to cover in 5-quart saucepan for 1 to 1 1/2 hours; drain. Add enough water to fill saucepan. Add potato, ham hocks, bacon, green pepper, onion, brown sugar and Cajun seasoning; mix well. Simmer for 1 hour, stirring occasionally. Add tomato soup. Bring to a boil. Boil for 5 minutes, stirring constantly. Reduce heat to low. Cook for 3 hours longer. Add extra water if soup becomes too thick.

Approx Per Serving: Cal 686; Prot 36 g; Carbo 69 g; Fiber 25 g; T Fat 30 g; Chol 50 mg; Sod 1309 mg.

ITALIAN SAUSAGE SOUP

| Yield: 8 servings | Utensil: soup pot | Preheat: no |

1 pound Italian sausage, chopped
1 pound ground pork
1 onion, chopped
1 28-ounce can tomatoes
1 15-ounce can tomato sauce
1 tomato sauce can water
1 14-ounce can chicken broth
3 zucchini, chopped
3/4 cup uncooked barley

Brown sausage and ground pork with onion in large skillet, stirring frequently; drain. Add to 8-quart soup pot with tomatoes, tomato sauce, water, chicken broth, zucchini and barley; mix well. Bring to a boil. Simmer for 30 minutes, stirring occasionally. Garnish individual servings with Parmesan cheese. May substitute broccoli or cauliflower for zucchini.

Approx Per Serving: Cal 285; Prot 21 g; Carbo 25 g; Fiber 5 g; T Fat 11 g; Chol 56 mg; Sod 894 mg.

POTATO SOUP WITH NOODLES

Yield: 8 servings　　　　Utensil: saucepan　　　　Preheat: no

4 potatoes
¾ cup sliced celery
¼ cup butter
1 quart milk
Salt and pepper to taste
1 quart chicken broth
1 egg
1 cup flour

Boil potatoes and celery together in medium saucepan until tender; drain. Mash potatoes; spoon into large saucepan. Add celery, butter, milk, salt, pepper and chicken broth; mix well. Mix egg and flour in small bowl. Shape into noodles. Add to soup. Simmer for 20 minutes, stirring frequently.

Approx Per Serving: Cal 314; Prot 11 g; Carbo 44 g; Fiber 3 g; T Fat 12 g; Chol 19 mg; Sod 511 mg.

POTATO SOUP WITH CHEESE AND BACON

Yield: 6 servings　　　　Utensil: saucepan　　　　Preheat: no

3 large potatoes, cubed
1 onion, chopped
1 stalk celery, chopped
¼ teaspoon salt
4½ cups milk
1½ tablespoons flour
⅓ cup water
1　12-ounce package bacon, crisp-fried, crumbled
8 ounces Velveeta cheese, cubed
⅛ teaspoon paprika
Salt and pepper to taste

Combine potatoes, onion and celery in 3-quart saucepan; cover with water. Add ¼ teaspoon salt. Cook over high heat until potatoes are tender. Drain, leaving ½ cup cooking water in saucepan. Mash potatoes with fork, adding milk gradually. Mix flour and ⅓ cup water in bowl until smooth. Add to potato mixture. Stir in bacon and cheese slowly. Add paprika, salt and pepper. Simmer for 30 minutes, stirring frequently.

Approx Per Serving: Cal 558; Prot 25 g; Carbo 37 g; Fiber 3 g; T Fat 35 g; Chol 93 mg; Sod 1085 mg.

Sauerkraut Soup

Yield: 8 servings   Utensil: soup pot   Preheat: no

1 46-ounce can chicken broth
5 carrots, thinly sliced
1 onion, chopped
3 stalks celery, sliced
8 ounces turkey summer sausage, sliced
3 chicken breasts, cooked, cubed
1 24-ounce jar sauerkraut
2 teaspoons dillweed
Salt and pepper to taste

Combine broth, carrots, onion, celery, summer sausage, chicken and sauerkraut in large soup pot. Stir in dillweed, salt and pepper to taste. Simmer for 6 to 8 hours, stirring occasionally. May add more chicken broth if needed.

Approx Per Serving: Cal 131; Prot 14 g; Carbo 11 g; Fiber 4 g; T Fat 3 g; Chol 28 mg; Sod 1233 mg.

Wild Rice Soup

Yield: 4 servings   Utensil: saucepan   Preheat: no

6 tablespoons butter
1 tablespoon minced onion
1/3 cup shredded carrot
1/2 cup flour
3 cups chicken broth
1/3 cup chopped ham
2 cups cooked wild rice
1/2 teaspoon salt
1 cup half and half
2 tablespoons sherry
3 tablespoons slivered almonds

Melt butter in saucepan. Add onion and carrot. Sauté until tender. Add flour, stirring until blended. Add chicken broth and ham; mix well. Bring mixture to a boil. Cook for 1 minute, stirring constantly. Add rice and salt. Simmer for 5 minutes, stirring constantly. Add half and half, sherry and almonds. Simmer until heated through. Serve hot, garnished with snipped parsley or chives.

Approx Per Serving: Cal 479; Prot 15 g; Carbo 37 g; Fiber 4 g; T Fat 30 g; Chol 76 mg; Sod 1178 mg.

Gourmet Vegetable Soup

Yield: 10 servings   Utensil: soup pot   Preheat: no

1½ quarts water
3 potatoes, peeled, chopped
3 carrots, peeled, sliced
1 onion, chopped
2 tablespoons parsley
3 chicken bouillon cubes
Pepper to taste
1 16-ounce package frozen mixed vegetables
2 10-ounce cans cream of mushroom soup
1 pound Velveeta cheese, cubed

Combine water, potatoes, carrots, onion, parsley, bouillon cubes and pepper in large soup pot. Simmer for 30 minutes or until potatoes are tender. Stir in frozen mixed vegetables. Cook for 30 minutes or until vegetables are tender. Remove from heat. Add soup and cheese, stirring until cheese is melted. Return to heat. Cook until warmed through. Serve with bread and salad.

Approx Per Serving: Cal 318; Prot 14 g; Carbo 25 g; Fiber 4 g; T Fat 19 g; Chol 44 mg; Sod 1514 mg.

Hot Chicken Sandwiches

Yield: 12 servings   Utensil: baking sheet   Preheat: 300 degrees

2 cups chopped cooked chicken
1 10-ounce can mushroom soup
2 cups prepared chicken gravy
1 2-ounce jar chopped pimento, drained
3 tablespoons chopped onion
1 8-ounce can sliced water chestnuts, drained
24 slices bread, crusts trimmed
4 eggs, beaten
1½ cups milk
2 cups crushed potato chips

Combine chicken, soup, gravy, pimento, onion and water chestnuts in bowl; mix well. Spoon filling onto 12 slices bread; cover with remaining 12 slices. Wrap individually with aluminum foil and freeze until ready to use. Dip each sandwich in mixture of eggs and milk; coat with crushed potato chips. Arrange on well greased baking sheet. Bake at 300 degrees for 1 hour.

Approx Per Serving: Cal 325; Prot 15 g; Carbo 38 g; Fiber 2 g; T Fat 12 g; Chol 93 mg; Sod 799 mg.

Pizza Burger

Yield: 20 servings	Utensil: skillet	Preheat: no

2 pounds ground beef
1 onion, chopped
1/2 cup water
1 16-ounce can pizza
    sauce
16 ounces Velveeta
    cheese, cubed
2 tablespoons Presti pizza
    mix
Dash of oregano
20 hamburger buns
1 1/2 cups shredded
    Cheddar cheese

Brown ground beef and onion in skillet, stirring until crumbly; drain. Add water. Simmer for 30 minutes, stirring frequently. Add pizza sauce, cheese, pizza mix and oregano. Simmer for 15 minutes or until cheese is melted and mixture is thickened, stirring constantly. Spoon onto hamburger buns. Top with cheese. Microwave on High for 1 minute or until cheese is melted.

Approx Per Serving: Cal 367; Prot 20 g; Carbo 27 g; Fiber 2 g;
    T Fat 20 g; Chol 60 mg; Sod 787 mg.
Nutritional information does not include pizza mix.

Stromboli Sandwich

Yield: 8 servings	Utensil: baking sheet	Preheat: 350 degrees

1 pound ground beef
2 tablespoons chopped
    onion
1/2 cup tomato sauce
3/4 cup catsup
1/4 teaspoon fennel seed
1/4 teaspoon oregano
1/2 teaspoon garlic powder
2 tablespoons grated
    Parmesan cheese
1 2 1/2-ounce can
    mushrooms, drained
1/4 cup butter, softened
1/2 teaspoon garlic powder
1/2 teaspoon paprika
1 16-ounce loaf French
    bread, sliced
    lengthwise
1 cup shredded
    mozzarella cheese

Brown ground beef and onion in skillet, stirring until crumbly; drain. Add tomato sauce, catsup, fennel seed, oregano, 1/2 teaspoon garlic powder, Parmesan cheese and mushrooms; mix well. Simmer for 20 minutes, stirring frequently. Mix butter, remaining 1/2 teaspoon garlic powder and paprika in small bowl. Spread over both halves of bread. Spoon ground beef mixture on half the bread. Sprinkle with mozzarella cheese. Top with remaining bread half. Wrap sandwich in aluminum foil; place on baking sheet. Bake at 350 degrees for 30 minutes. Serve hot.

Approx Per Serving: Cal 408; Prot 20 g; Carbo 37 g; Fiber 2 g;
    T Fat 19 g; Chol 65 mg; Sod 883 mg.

Tasty Tuna Crescents

Yield: 8 servings   Utensil: baking sheet   Preheat: 375 degrees

3 ounces cream cheese, softened
2 tablespoons Italian salad dressing mix
1 teaspoon onion powder
1 teaspoon dillweed
1 7-ounce can tuna, drained
1 8-count can crescent rolls
1 tablespoon margarine, melted

Combine cream cheese, salad dressing mix, onion powder and dillweed in small bowl; mix well. Stir in tuna. Separate crescent roll dough into 8 triangles. Place 1 heaping tablespoon tuna mixture on widest part of triangle. Fold up to cover tuna; press seams to seal. Place seam side down on ungreased baking sheet. Brush with melted margarine. Garnish with sesame seeds or Parmesan cheese. Bake at 375 degrees for 12 to 17 minutes or until golden brown.

Approx Per Serving: Cal 182; Prot 9 g; Carbo 10 g; Fiber <1 g; T Fat 12 g; Chol 26 mg; Sod 344 mg.

Taco Sandwiches

Yield: 5 servings   Utensil: skillet   Preheat: no

1 16-ounce loaf frozen bread dough, thawed
1 onion, chopped
1 tablespoon vegetable oil
1½ pounds ground beef
1½ envelopes Taco seasoning mix
1 15-ounce can chili beans
Oil for frying
½ head lettuce, shredded
3 tomatoes, chopped
8 ounces Cheddar cheese, shredded

Let bread dough rise following package directions. Divide into 10 equal portions. Roll out into 6-inch circles. Place between waxed paper; set aside. Sauté onion in 1 tablespoon oil in skillet. Add ground beef. Cook until ground beef is browned and crumbly, stirring frequently; drain. Add taco seasoning mix and water using package directions. Add chili beans. Simmer for 30 minutes, stirring frequently. Spoon ground beef mixture onto 1 side of each bread dough circle. Fold dough over, sealing edges. Fry in 2-inches hot oil in skillet, turning once to brown. Open along seamed edge. Sprinkle with lettuce, tomatoes and cheese.

Approx Per Serving: Cal 797; Prot 46 g; Carbo 59 g; Fiber 4 g; T Fat 42 g; Chol 137 mg; Sod 1872 mg.
Nutritional information does not include oil for frying.

Salads

APRICOT SALAD WITH TOPPING

Yield: 9 servings   Utensil: glass dish   Preheat: no

1 6-ounce package orange gelatin
2 cups boiling water
1 cup apricot syrup
2 cups chopped apricots
2 cups crushed pineapple
1 cup apricot syrup
1/4 cup sugar
2 tablespoons flour
1 egg, beaten
1 cup whipping cream, whipped

Dissolve gelatin in boiling water in bowl. Add 1 cup apricot syrup, apricots and undrained pineapple; mix well. Pour into 9x9-inch glass dish. Chill until firm. Combine remaining 1 cup apricot syrup, sugar, flour and egg in saucepan. Cook over medium heat until thickened, stirring constantly. Let stand until cool. Fold in whipped cream gently. Spread over congealed layer. Chill before serving.

Approx Per Serving: Cal 284; Prot 4 g; Carbo 47 g; Fiber 1 g; T Fat 11 g; Chol 60 mg; Sod 80 mg.

CRANBERRY-CHERRY SALAD

Yield: 8 servings   Utensil: dish   Preheat: no

1 6-ounce package cherry gelatin
1 3-ounce package cherry gelatin
1 1/2 cups boiling water
1 cup sour cream
1 16-ounce can whole cranberry sauce
1 16-ounce can cranberry-orange relish
1/2 cup chopped walnuts

Dissolve gelatins in boiling water in bowl. Chill until partially set. Add sour cream, stirring until creamy. Stir in cranberry sauce, cranberry-orange relish and walnuts. Pour into 9x13-inch dish. Chill until set.

Approx Per Serving: Cal 414; Prot 5 g; Carbo 79 g; Fiber 3 g; T Fat 11 g; Chol 13 mg; Sod 152 mg.

Fruity Cheese Salad

Yield: 8 servings   Utensil: mold   Preheat: no

1½ envelopes unflavored gelatin
½ cup cold water
1 8-ounce can crushed pineapple
¾ cup sugar
3 tablespoons lemon juice
1 cup shredded American cheese
½ cup sliced stuffed olives
1 cup whipped cream

Soak gelatin in cold water. Drain pineapple, reserving liquid. Add enough water to reserved pineapple liquid to make 1 cup. Bring sugar, reserved pineapple liquid and lemon juice to a boil in saucepan. Cook until sugar is dissolved, stirring constantly. Add gelatin and pineapple; mix well. Chill until partially set. Stir in cheese, olives and whipped cream. Pour into 6-cup mold. Chill until set. Unmold onto serving plate.

Approx Per Serving: Cal 221; Prot 5 g; Carbo 26 g; Fiber 1 g; T Fat 12 g; Chol 34 mg; Sod 550 mg.

Fruit Basket Upset

Yield: 6 servings   Utensil: serving bowl   Preheat: no

1 8-ounce can fruit cocktail, drained
2 bananas, sliced
1 small apple, chopped
½ cup seedless grape halves
¼ cup sliced maraschino cherries
½ cup sliced strawberries
¼ cup miniature marshmallows
½ cup whipping cream, whipped
1 or 2 drops of red food coloring

Combine fruit cocktail, bananas, apple, grapes, cherries, strawberries and marshmallows in a large bowl; mix well. Tint whipped cream with 1 or 2 drops of red food coloring. Fold into fruit mixture gently. Spoon into serving bowl. Chill before serving. Garnish with fresh strawberries and white grapes. May add fresh pineapple to fruit mixture.

Approx Per Serving: Cal 170; Prot 1 g; Carbo 27 g; Fiber 2 g; T Fat 8 g; Chol 27 mg; Sod 13 mg.

Golden Fleck Salad

Yield: 20 servings   Utensil: serving dish   Preheat: no

1 envelope unflavored gelatin
¼ cup cold water
2 6-ounce packages lemon gelatin
3 cups boiling water
2 tablespoons lemon juice
1 cup pineapple juice
1 cup miniature marshmallows
8 ounces cream cheese, softened
2 cups crushed pineapple, drained
½ cup chopped pecans
2 cups grated carrots
8 ounces whipped topping

Soften unflavored gelatin in cold water. Dissolve lemon gelatin and softened gelatin in boiling water in large mixer bowl. Add lemon juice, pineapple juice, marshmallows and cream cheese; beat until smooth. Let stand until cool. Stir in pineapple, pecans and carrots. Fold in whipped topping gently. Spoon into serving dish. Chill before serving.

Approx Per Serving: Cal 179; Prot 3 g; Carbo 24 g; Fiber 1 g; T Fat 9 g; Chol 12 mg; Sod 82 mg.

Double Lemon Salad

Yield: 12 servings   Utensil: serving bowl   Preheat: no

1 6-ounce package lemon gelatin
2 cups boiling water
1 21-ounce can lemon pie filling
½ cup cold water
1 20-ounce can crushed pineapple

Dissolve gelatin in boiling water in bowl. Add pie filling. Beat with an egg beater. Stir in cold water and undrained pineapple. Pour into serving bowl. Chill until serving time.

Approx Per Serving: Cal 137; Prot 2 g; Carbo 34 g; Fiber 1 g; T Fat <1 g; Chol 0 mg; Sod 60 mg.

LIME-CHEESE SALAD

Yield: 9 servings   Utensil: dish   Preheat: no

6 ounces cream cheese, softened
1 cup mayonnaise
1 cup milk
1 3-ounce package lime gelatin
½ cup boiling water
1 8-ounce can crushed pineapple
½ cup chopped pecans

Beat cream cheese in bowl until smooth. Add mayonnaise and milk; mix well. Add gelatin dissolved in boiling water. Stir in pineapple and pecans. Pour into 8-inch square dish. Chill until set.

Approx Per Serving: Cal 350; Prot 11 g; Carbo 8 g; Fiber 2 g; T Fat 31 g; Chol 39 mg; Sod 215 mg.

PEACH AMBROSIA SALAD

Yield: 18 servings   Utensil: dish   Preheat: no

1 cup water
1 cup sugar
1 20-ounce can crushed pineapple
1 6-ounce package peach gelatin
8 ounces cream cheese, softened
5 tablespoons milk
8 ounces whipped topping

Combine water, sugar and undrained pineapple in saucepan. Bring to a boil. Remove from heat. Stir in gelatin until dissolved. Let stand until cool. Beat cream cheese and milk in bowl until smooth. Fold in whipped topping. Stir in gelatin mixture. Pour into 9x13-inch dish. Chill overnight.

Approx Per Serving: Cal 183; Prot 2 g; Carbo 28 g; Fiber <1 g; T Fat 8 g; Chol 14 mg; Sod 73 mg.

Quick Sunny Salad

Yield: 8 servings Utensil: large bowl Preheat: no

1 11-ounce can mandarin oranges
1 8-ounce can crushed pineapple
2 cups miniature marshmallows
2 cups whipped topping
1 cup coconut
1 4-ounce package French vanilla instant pudding mix

Combine mandarin oranges, pineapple, miniature marshmallows, whipped topping, coconut and pudding mix in large bowl; mix well. Chill until serving time. May add 1 cup chopped pecans if desired.

Approx Per Serving: Cal 248; Prot 1 g; Carbo 46 g; Fiber 2 g; T Fat 8 g; Chol 0 mg; Sod 117 mg.

Raspberry Salad

Yield: 6 servings Utensil: glass dish Preheat: no

1 3-ounce package raspberry gelatin
1/2 cup plus 2 tablespoons boiling water
1 10-ounce package frozen raspberries, partially thawed
1 cup applesauce
1 cup sour cream
1 cup miniature marshmallows

Dissolve gelatin in boiling water in bowl. Add raspberries and applesauce; mix well. Pour into 6x10-inch glass dish. Chill until set. Combine sour cream and marshmallows in small bowl. Let stand for 15 minutes. Spread over congealed layer. Chill until serving time.

Approx Per Serving: Cal 231; Prot 3 g; Carbo 39 g; Fiber 3 g; T Fat 8 g; Chol 17 mg; Sod 75 mg.

Corned Beef Salad

Yield: 12 servings   Utensil: glass dish   Preheat: no

1 6-ounce package lemon gelatin
Salt to taste
1¾ cups boiling water
3 tablespoons lemon juice
1 12-ounce can corned beef, shredded
2 hard-cooked eggs, chopped
1 cup chopped cucumber
½ cup chopped green bell pepper
1½ cups chopped celery
¼ cup minced onion
2 teaspoons pimento
1 cup mayonnaise-type salad dressing

Dissolve gelatin and salt in boiling water in bowl. Let stand to cool. Stir in lemon juice. Combine corned beef, eggs, cucumber, green pepper, celery, onion, pimento and mayonnaise in large bowl; mix well. Pour into 9x13-inch glass dish. Chill until set. Garnish with green bell pepper rings or olives. May substitute mayonnaise-type salad dressing for mayonnaise.

Approx Per Serving: Cal 221; Prot 11 g; Carbo 19 g; Fiber 1 g; T Fat 12 g; Chol 65 mg; Sod 495 mg.

Fruited Chicken Salad

Yield: 10 servings   Utensil: serving bowl   Preheat: no

4 cups cubed cooked chicken
1 15-ounce can pineapple chunks, drained
1 11-ounce can mandarin oranges, drained
1 cup finely chopped celery
1½ cups seedless grapes
1 cup slivered almonds
1¼ cups mayonnaise
½ teaspoon salt
1 teaspoon tarragon
1 teaspoon dry mustard

Combine chicken, pineapple, mandarin oranges, celery, grapes and almonds in serving bowl; mix well. Blend mayonnaise, salt, tarragon and dry mustard in small bowl. Pour over chicken mixture; mix well. Chill for 2 hours before serving.

Approx Per Serving: Cal 423; Prot 17 g; Carbo 19 g; Fiber 3 g; T Fat 33 g; Chol 57 mg; Sod 317 mg.

IMMC Chicken Salad with Fruit

Yield: 4 servings　　Utensil: serving bowl　　Preheat: no

3 cups chopped cooked chicken
1½ tablespoons toasted slivered almonds
¾ cup pineapple tidbits, drained
¾ cup seedless grape halves
1½ tablespoons chopped celery
1½ tablespoons light mayonnaise-type salad dressing
⅔ cup plain low-fat yogurt
1¼ teaspoons horseradish

Combine chicken, almonds, pineapple, grapes and celery in serving bowl; mix well. Blend salad dressing, yogurt and horseradish in small bowl. Pour over chicken mixture; toss to mix. Chill for at least 3 hours. Salad may appear dry at first but will moisten after chilling.

Approx Per Serving: Cal 392; Prot 39 g; Carbo 17 g; Fiber 1 g; T Fat 18 g; Chol 102 mg; Sod 169 mg.

Summer Pasta Salad

Yield: 6 servings　　Utensil: mixer bowl　　Preheat: no

1 16-ounce package rainbow pasta
¾ cup mustard
1 cup shredded sharp Cheddar cheese
¼ cup thinly sliced green olives
2 cups finely chopped tomatoes
⅓ cup bacon bits

Cook pasta using package directions, rinsing 2 times; drain well. Combine with mustard in mixer bowl; mix well. Add cheese, olives and tomatoes; mix well. Stir in bacon bits. Chill for 1 hour before serving.

Approx Per Serving: Cal 425; Prot 16 g; Carbo 64 g; Fiber 6 g; T Fat 12 g; Chol 20 mg; Sod 887 mg.

Wild Rice Salad

Yield: 10 servings   Utensil: salad bowl   Preheat: no

5 cups cooked wild rice
¾ cup sliced green onions
¾ cup chopped celery
½ cup toasted slivered almonds
3 tablespoons safflower oil
3 tablespoons olive oil
3 tablespoons white wine vinegar
1 tablespoon thyme
1 teaspoon rosemary
½ teaspoon salt
¼ teaspoon pepper

Combine rice, green onions, celery and almonds in salad bowl; mix well. Add safflower oil and olive oil 1 drop at a time to vinegar in small bowl, whisking until blended. Stir in thyme, rosemary, salt and pepper. Pour over rice; toss to mix. Chill until serving time.

Approx Per Serving: Cal 208; Prot 5 g; Carbo 21 g; Fiber 4 g; T Fat 12 g; Chol 0 mg; Sod 118 mg.

Caesar Vegetable Salad

Yield: 10 servings   Utensil: salad bowl   Preheat: no

1 12-ounce package frozen peas
1 bunch broccoli, chopped
1 head cauliflower, chopped
1 bunch green onions, sliced
1 cup chopped celery
1 8-ounce can water chestnuts, sliced
1 8-ounce bottle of Caesar salad dressing

Combine peas, broccoli, cauliflower, green onions, celery and water chestnuts in salad bowl. Pour salad dressing over mixture; toss to mix. May substitute vegetable dip mix and 1½ cups mayonnaise for Caesar salad dressing.

Approx Per Serving: Cal 162; Prot 6 g; Carbo 13 g; Fiber 5 g; T Fat 11 g; Chol 27 mg; Sod 279 mg.

BACON AND CAULIFLOWER SALAD

Yield: 10 servings   Utensil: salad bowl   Preheat: no

1 head lettuce, torn
1 head cauliflower, chopped
1 pound bacon, crisp-fried, crumbled
1 onion, chopped
1/3 cup Parmesan cheese
1/4 cup sugar
1 cup mayonnaise
Salt and pepper to taste

Combine lettuce, cauliflower, bacon and onion in salad bowl. Blend Parmesan cheese, sugar and mayonnaise in small bowl. Pour over vegetable mixture; toss to mix. Add salt and pepper to taste. Chill for 2 hours before serving.

Approx Per Serving: Cal 280; Prot 7 g; Carbo 8 g; Fiber 1 g; T Fat 25 g; Chol 27 mg; Sod 400 mg.

FRESH CAULIFLOWER AND BROCCOLI SALAD

Yield: 10 servings   Utensil: salad bowl   Preheat: no

2 cups finely chopped fresh broccoli
2 cups finely chopped fresh cauliflower
2 tablespoons chopped onion
1 teaspoon pepper
1 1/2 cups shredded Cheddar cheese
1/2 cup chopped celery
1 1/4 cups mayonnaise-type salad dressing
3 to 4 tablespoons milk
3/4 cup sliced radishes
1 cup frozen peas

Combine broccoli, cauliflower, onion, pepper, cheese, celery, salad dressing, milk, radishes and peas in salad bowl; mix well. Chill, covered, in refrigerator.

Approx Per Serving: Cal 211; Prot 7 g; Carbo 12 g; Fiber 2 g; T Fat 16 g; Chol 26 mg; Sod 350 mg.

COLONEL SANDER'S COLESLAW

Yield: 8 servings   Utensil: salad bowl   Preheat: no

3 cups shredded cabbage
½ cup finely shredded carrots
¼ cup milk
2 tablespoons sugar
Dash of salt
½ cup mayonnaise
¼ cup buttermilk
¼ teaspoon celery seed
2 or 3 drops of Tabasco sauce
1 tablespoon onion flakes

Combine cabbage, carrots, milk, sugar and salt in salad bowl; toss with 2 forks. Chill, covered, for at least 1 hour. Combine mayonnaise, buttermilk, celery seed, Tabasco sauce and onion flakes in small bowl; mix until smooth. Pour over chilled cabbage mixture; toss using 2 forks. Chill until serving time.

Approx Per Serving: Cal 127; Prot 1 g; Carbo 6 g; Fiber 1 g; T Fat 11 g; Chol 9 mg; Sod 96 mg.

ORIENTAL COLESLAW

Yield: 8 servings   Utensil: salad bowl   Preheat: 350 degrees

2 tablespoons sesame seed
½ cup slivered almonds
4 cups shredded cabbage
3 green onions, sliced
3 ounces ramen noodles, crumbled
3 tablespoons sugar
½ teaspoon pepper
½ cup oil

Place sesame seed and slivered almonds on baking sheet. Toast in 350-degree oven for 10 minutes. Let stand to cool. Combine cabbage and onions in salad bowl. Reserve seasoning packet from ramen noodles. Add ramen noodles to cabbage mixture; toss. Mix sugar, pepper, oil and ramen seasoning mix in covered container; shake well. Add sesame seed and almonds to cabbage mixture; pour salad dressing over top. Toss to mix. Serve immediately. May make recipe in advance by combining all ingredients except ramen noodles and salad dressing. Chill until ready to serve.

Approx Per Serving: Cal 253; Prot 4 g; Carbo 17 g; Fiber 3 g; T Fat 20 g; Chol 0 mg; Sod 223 mg.

Go-With-Everything Salad

Yield: 12 servings   Utensil: salad bowl   Preheat: no

1 cup sugar
¾ cup vinegar
½ cup vegetable oil
1 teaspoon celery seed
Salt and pepper to taste
1 16-ounce can French-style green beans, drained
1 16-ounce can white corn, drained
¾ cup chopped green onions
1 16-ounce can tiny peas, drained
1 4-ounce jar pimentos, drained
1 4-ounce jar sliced mushrooms, drained
1 cup chopped celery
¾ cup chopped green bell pepper

Combine sugar, vinegar, oil, celery seed, salt and pepper in saucepan. Cook over low heat until sugar and salt are dissolved, stirring frequently. Let stand until cool. Combine green beans, corn, green onions, peas, pimentos, mushrooms, celery and green peppers in salad bowl; toss well. Pour cooled dressing over vegetables; toss well. Chill for 8 hours to overnight before serving.

Approx Per Serving: Cal 213; Prot 3 g; Carbo 32 g; Fiber 4 g; T Fat 10 g; Chol 0 mg; Sod 323 mg.

Layered Lettuce Salad

Yield: 20 servings   Utensil: large bowl   Preheat: no

1 head lettuce, chopped
1 onion, chopped
1 pound bacon, crisp-fried, crumbled
1 head cauliflower, chopped
¼ cup sugar
2 cups mayonnaise-type salad dressing
⅓ cup grated Parmesan cheese

Layer lettuce, onion, bacon, cauliflower, sugar, salad dressing and Parmesan cheese in large bowl. Chill, covered, until serving time. Toss just before serving.

Approx Per Serving: Cal 155; Prot 3 g; Carbo 10 g; Fiber 1 g; T Fat 12 g; Chol 13 mg; Sod 304 mg.

Lauri's Tossed Salad

| Yield: 8 servings | Utensil: salad bowl | Preheat: no |

1 head romaine lettuce, torn
1 head iceberg lettuce, torn
1 red onion, sliced
12 to 15 cherry tomatoes
2 tablespoons sunflower seed
1/2 cup bleu cheese
1 cup croutons
1 avocado, sliced
3 tablespoons mayonnaise
1 tablespoon prepared horseradish
1 tablespoon prepared mustard
1/4 cup olive oil
1/4 cup tarragon or balsamic vinegar

Combine romaine lettuce, iceberg lettuce, onion, tomatoes, sunflower seed, bleu cheese, croutons and avocado in salad bowl; toss. Combine mayonnaise, horseradish, mustard, oil and vinegar in small bowl; blend well. Pour over salad; toss again.

Approx Per Serving: Cal 215; Prot 4 g; Carbo 11 g; Fiber 4 g; T Fat 18 g; Chol 8 mg; Sod 215 mg.

Mom's Best Potato Salad

| Yield: 10 servings | Utensil: salad bowl | Preheat: no |

1 1/2 cups mayonnaise-type salad dressing
1 1/4 teaspoons pickle juice
1 1/2 tablespoons milk
1/4 teaspoon yellow food coloring
2 teaspoons celery salt
1 teaspoon sugar
10 to 15 cooked peeled potatoes, chopped

Combine salad dressing, pickle juice, milk, food coloring, celery salt, pickle relish and sugar in bowl; mix well. Pour over potatoes in bowl; mix well. Spoon into lettuce-lined salad bowl. Chill until serving time. May substitute 1 1/2 cups mayonnaise for mayonnaise-type salad dressing or add pickle relish if desired.

Approx Per Serving: Cal 356; Prot 5 g; Carbo 59 g; Fiber 4 g; T Fat 12 g; Chol 9 mg; Sod 690 mg.

Spinach Salad with Mustard-Bacon Dressing

Yield: 12 servings Utensil: salad bowl Preheat: no

1 cup mayonnaise
1 small onion, finely grated
¼ cup vegetable oil
¼ cup red wine vinegar
3 tablespoons sugar
1 tablespoon Dijon-style mustard
Salt and pepper to taste
3 tablespoons bacon drippings
2 pounds spinach
1½ pounds mushrooms, sliced
6 hard-cooked eggs, sliced, chilled
1 pound bacon, crisp-fried, crumbled
½ cup grated Parmesan cheese

Combine mayonnaise, onion, oil, vinegar, sugar, mustard, salt and pepper in small bowl; mix well. Stir in bacon drippings. Wash spinach; remove stems. Tear into bite-sized pieces. Combine with mushrooms and eggs in salad bowl. Pour mayonnaise mixture over salad; toss gently. Sprinkle with cooled bacon crumbs and Parmesan cheese. May make salad dressing 2 days before serving.

Approx Per Serving: Cal 371; Prot 12 g; Carbo 11 g; Fiber 4 g; T Fat 33 g; Chol 151 mg; Sod 496 mg.

Strawberry-Spinach Salad

Yield: 6 servings Utensil: salad bowl Preheat: no

1   10-ounce package fresh spinach
1 pound fresh strawberries, cut into halves
¼ cup sugar
Juice of 1 large lemon
1 egg yolk
6 tablespoons vegetable oil

Wash spinach and remove stems; tear into pieces. Arrange spinach in salad bowl; top with strawberries. Chill until serving time. Whisk sugar and lemon juice in small bowl until most of the sugar is dissolved. Add egg yolk, whisking until sugar is completely dissolved. Add oil 1 tablespoonful at a time, whisking constantly until thickened and creamy. Chill, covered, in refrigerator. Whisk salad dressing before serving. Pour over salad; toss gently to mix well.

Approx Per Serving: Cal 198; Prot 2 g; Carbo 16 g; Fiber 4 g; T Fat 15 g; Chol 36 mg; Sod 40 mg.

IMMC Spinach Leaf Salad

Yield: 1 servingUtensil: salad platePreheat: no

2 cups fresh spinach, torn
2 tablespoons crumbled crisp-fried bacon
1 teaspoon grated Parmesan cheese
1/4 cup seasoned croutons
3 red onion rings
1/2 hard-cooked egg, cut into 3 wedges
1 black olive
1 1-ounce slice provolone cheese, cut into strips
1/4 cup IMMC Homemade Italian Salad Dressing

Wash spinach; remove stems. Place spinach on salad plate. Top with bacon, Parmesan cheese, croutons and onion rings. Arrange egg wedges, black olive and strips of provolone cheese on salad. Serve with salad dressing.

Approx Per Serving: Cal 1069 Prot 22 g; Carbo 39 g; Fiber 3 g; T Fat 96 g; Chol 170 mg; Sod 1543 mg.

IMMC Homemade Italian Salad Dressing

Yield: 20 servingsUtensil: medium bowlPreheat: no

3 cups corn oil
1 cup red wine vinegar
1 cup lemon juice
1 tablespoon plus 1 teaspoon crushed garlic
1 teaspoon pepper
2 teaspoons salt
2 teaspoons tarragon
2 teaspoons ground oregano

Combine oil, vinegar, lemon juice, garlic, pepper, salt, tarragon and oregano in medium bowl; mix well. Store, covered, in refrigerator.

Approx Per Serving: Cal 295; Prot <1 g; Carbo 2 g; Fiber <1 g; T Fat 33 g; Chol 0 mg; Sod 214 mg.

Easy Bleu Cheese Dressing

Yield: 50 servings Utensil: mixer bowl Preheat: no

1 32-ounce jar mayonnaise
1 cup sour cream
1 tablespoon garlic powder
4 ounces bleu cheese
1 tablespoon grated onion
Salt and pepper to taste

Combine mayonnaise, sour cream, garlic powder, bleu cheese, onion, salt and pepper in mixer bowl. Beat until smooth. Spoon into 1½-quart container. Store, covered, in refrigerator.

Approx Per Serving: Cal 144; Prot 1 g; Carbo 1 g; Fiber <1 g; T Fat 16 g; Chol 14 mg; Sod 134 mg.

Salad Dressing for Coleslaw

Yield: 30 servings Utensil: small saucepan Preheat: no

1 tablespoon unflavored gelatin
¼ cup cold water
1 cup vinegar
1½ cups sugar
1 teaspoon celery seed
1 teaspoon salt
¼ teaspoon pepper
1 cup salad oil

Soften gelatin in cold water. Combine vinegar, sugar, celery seed, salt and pepper in small saucepan. Cook over medium heat until almost boiling. Remove from heat. Stir in softened gelatin. Let stand until of the consistency of cream. Add salad oil; beat well. Store, covered, in refrigerator.

Approx Per Serving: Cal 105; Prot <1 g; Carbo 10 g; Fiber <1 g; T Fat 7 g; Chol 0 mg; Sod 72 mg.

Honey Salad Dressing

Yield: 30 servings Utensil: blender Preheat: no

⅔ cup sugar
1 teaspoon dry mustard
1 teaspoon paprika
¼ teaspoon salt
1 teaspoon celery seed
5 tablespoons vinegar
3 tablespoons lemon juice
1 teaspoon grated onion
1 cup strained honey
½ cup salad oil

Combine sugar, dry mustard, paprika, salt, celery seed, vinegar, lemon juice and onion in blender container. Process until sugar is dissolved. Add honey. Process until blended. Add oil in fine steam, processing at high speed until completely blended. Store, covered, in refrigerator. Serve on fruit salads.

Approx Per Serving: Cal 84; Prot <1 g; Carbo 14 g; Fiber <1 g; T Fat 4 g; Chol 0 mg; Sod 19 mg.

Meat and Meatless Main Dishes

Gourmet Beef and Lobster

Yield: 12 servings   Utensil: baking pan   Preheat: 400 degrees

1 4-pound beef tenderloin
2 whole lobster tails, cooked, shelled, chopped
1 cup butter, melted
2 tablespoons lemon juice
3 tablespoons parsley
¼ cup minced onion

Make a slit along one side of tenderloin to form pocket. Spoon chopped lobster meat inside. Tie with string to securely close opening. Place in baking pan. Mix butter, lemon juice, parsley and onion in small bowl. Drizzle ½ of the butter sauce over tenderloin. Bake at 400 degrees for 30 minutes or until desired degree of doneness. Serve with remaining butter sauce.

Approx Per Serving: Cal 361; Prot 34 g; Carbo 1 g; Fiber <1 g; T Fat 24 g; Chol 153 mg; Sod 261 mg.

Pepper Steak

Yield: 6 servings   Utensil: skillet   Preheat: no

1 pound beef chuck, cut into thin strips
¼ cup vegetable oil
1 clove of garlic, minced
1 tablespoon soy sauce
1 teaspoon salt
¼ cup water
1 cup green bell pepper strips
½ cup chopped onion
1 tablespoon cornstarch
1 cup water
2 tomatoes, chopped

Brown strips of chuck in hot oil in skillet. Add garlic; sauté until golden. Add soy sauce, salt and ¼ cup water. Simmer, covered, for 45 minutes, stirring occasionally. Add green pepper and onion. Simmer for 10 minutes longer. Blend cornstarch and 1 cup water. Stir into mixture slowly. Cook until thickened, stirring constantly. Add tomatoes. Simmer for 5 minutes longer. Serve over hot rice.

Approx Per Serving: Cal 202; Prot 15 g; Carbo 5 g; Fiber 1 g; T Fat 14 g; Chol 43 mg; Sod 554 mg.

Easy Pepper Steak

| Yield: 4 servings | Utensil: skillet | Preheat: yes |

1½ pounds round steak, cut into 2-inch strips
2 cups water
1 envelope onion soup mix
1 green bell pepper, cut into thin strips
1½ tablespoons cornstarch
½ cup water

Stir-fry round steak in hot skillet. Add 2 cups water and onion soup mix; mix well. Simmer, covered, for 1 hour, stirring occasionally. Add green pepper. Simmer, covered, for 30 minutes longer. Blend cornstarch with ½ cup water. Add to mixture. Cook until thickened, stirring constantly. Serve over rice.

Approx Per Serving: Cal 245; Prot 32 g; Carbo 5 g; Fiber <1 g; T Fat 10 g; Chol 96 mg; Sod 210 mg.

Onion-Buttered Sirloin

| Yield: 6 servings | Utensil: broiler pan | Preheat: broiler |

1 4-pound sirloin, 1½ inches thick
½ cup butter
¼ cup chopped parsley
¼ cup minced onion
2 teaspoons Worcestershire sauce
½ teaspoon dry mustard
½ teaspoon pepper

Score edges of sirloin at 1-inch intervals. Place on broiler pan. Combine butter, parsley, onion, Worcestershire sauce, mustard and pepper in saucepan. Heat until butter is melted, stirring constantly. Brush mixture on sirloin. Broil for 5 minutes; turn. Baste with butter mixture. Broil for 2 minutes longer or to desired degree of doneness. Drizzle remaining butter mixture over individual servings.

Approx Per Serving: Cal 538; Prot 57 g; Carbo 1 g; Fiber <1 g; T Fat 33 g; Chol 212 mg; Sod 239 mg.

Sunday Roast

Yield: 10 servings　　Utensil: roasting pan　　Preheat: 300 degrees

1　4-pound beef roast
2　tablespoons Worcestershire sauce
1　10-ounce can cream of mushroom soup
1　envelope onion soup mix

Place roast in aluminum foil-lined roasting pan. Sprinkle with Worcestershire sauce. Pour mixture of cream of mushroom soup and onion soup mix over roast. Seal aluminum foil around roast. Bake at 300 degrees for 1 hour. Bake at 200 degrees for 4 hours longer. Serve with new potatoes and carrots.

Approx Per Serving: Cal 273; Prot 32 g; Carbo 3 g; Fiber <1 g; T Fat 16 g; Chol 105 mg; Sod 373 mg.

Marinated Shish Kabob

Yield: 4 servings　　Utensil: broiler pan　　Preheat: broiler

2 pounds lean beef, cubed
1 teaspoon salt
1 teaspoon pepper
3 tablespoons chopped fresh parsley
1/2 teaspoon thyme
1/2 teaspoon oregano
1 bay leaf
2 cloves of garlic
3/4 cup olive oil
3/4 cup red wine

Place beef cubes in shallow dish. Sprinkle with salt, pepper, parsley, thyme and oregano. Add bay leaf and garlic. Stir in oil and wine. Marinate beef at room temperature for 4 to 5 hours or in refrigerator overnight; drain. Thread beef cubes onto skewers. Place on rack in broiler pan or over hot coals. Broil or grill until done to taste.

Approx Per Serving: Cal 687; Prot 42 g; Carbo 1 g; Fiber 0 g; T Fat 53 g; Chol 128 mg; Sod 605 mg.

SLOW-COOKING STEW

Yield: 6 servings   Utensil: roasting pan   Preheat: 250 degrees

1½ pounds stew meat, trimmed
8 onions
1½ teaspoons salt
1 teaspoon sugar
½ cup soft bread crumbs
1 16-ounce can tomatoes
1 cup chopped celery
4 carrots, chopped
3 tablespoons quick tapioca

Place stew meat and onions in roasting pan. Sprinkle with salt, sugar and bread crumbs. Add tomatoes, celery and carrots. Stir in tapioca. Roast, covered, at 250 degrees for 5 hours, stirring twice. May add red wine and additional vegetables.

Approx Per Serving: Cal 297; Prot 26 g; Carbo 33 g; Fiber 7 g; T Fat 7 g; Chol 64 mg; Sod 1083 mg.

REUBEN CASSEROLE

Yield: 10 servings   Utensil: casserole   Preheat: 350 degrees

2 10-ounce cans cream of chicken soup
1¾ cups milk
½ cup chopped onion
1 tablespoon prepared mustard
2 16-ounce jars sauerkraut, drained
1 8-ounce package noodles
1 12-ounce can corned beef, crumbled
2 cups shredded Swiss cheese
¾ cup rye bread crumbs
3 tablespoons margarine, melted

Combine soup, milk, onion and mustard in bowl; mix well. Layer sauerkraut, noodles, soup mixture, corned beef and cheese in greased 9x13-inch casserole. Toss bread crumbs with melted butter. Sprinkle over top layer. Bake, covered, at 350 degrees for 1 hour or until noodles are tender. May substitute cream of mushroom soup for chicken soup.

Approx Per Serving: Cal 402; Prot 23 g; Carbo 30 g; Fiber 2 g; T Fat 21 g; Chol 61 mg; Sod 1588 mg.

Beefy Spinach and Cheese Cassata

Yield: 8 servings   Utensil: springform pan   Preheat: 350 degrees

2 pounds ground beef
1/2 cup chopped onion
1/2 cup chopped green bell pepper
1 clove of garlic, minced
3/4 teaspoon salt
1 8-ounce can tomato sauce
1 6-ounce can tomato paste
1/3 cup white wine
2 teaspoons dried oregano
1/4 teaspoon pepper
1/4 cup bread crumbs
1/4 cup grated Parmesan cheese
1 clove of garlic, minced
1 tablespoon margarine
1 10-ounce package frozen chopped spinach, thawed, drained
2 eggs, beaten
1 cup ricotta cheese
1 cup shredded mozzarella cheese
1/2 cup grated Parmesan cheese
1 16-ounce package phyllo pastry leaves
1/3 cup melted margarine
2 tablespoons grated Parmesan cheese

Brown ground beef with onion, green pepper and 1 clove of garlic in skillet, stirring until ground beef is crumbly; drain. Sprinkle with salt. Add tomato sauce, tomato paste, wine, oregano and pepper to ground beef mixture; mix well. Simmer for 5 minutes, stirring frequently. Stir in bread crumbs and 1/4 cup Parmesan cheese; set aside. Brown remaining clove of garlic in 1 tablespoon margarine in saucepan. Add spinach. Simmer, covered, for 5 minutes. Remove from heat. Add eggs, ricotta cheese, mozzarella cheese and remaining 1/2 cup Parmesan cheese; mix well. Line 9-inch springform pan with 6 phyllo leaves, overlapping edges. Spoon in ground beef mixture, pressing down lightly. Top with spinach mixture. Fold phyllo leaves over top; brush with melted margarine. Cut four 9-inch circles from remaining phyllo leaves. Place one circle over top, brush with melted margarine. Repeat with remaining 3 circles. Cut through leaves to make 8 wedges. Bake at 350 degrees for 30 minutes. Sprinkle with remaining 2 tablespoons Parmesan cheese. Bake for 5 minutes longer or until golden brown. Let stand for 5 to 10 minutes. Remove sides of pan.

Approx Per Serving: Cal 670; Prot 41 g; Carbo 49 g; Fiber 5 g; T Fat 33 g; Chol 158 mg; Sod 1073 mg.

Mexican Casserole

Yield: 6 servings Utensil: baking dish Preheat: 350 degrees

1 pound ground beef
1 4-ounce can chopped green chilies, drained
1 envelope taco seasoning mix
1 10-ounce can tomato soup
2 cups cooked rice
2 cups chopped tomatoes
2 cups shredded Cheddar cheese
1 cup crushed corn chips

Brown ground beef in skillet, stirring until crumbly; drain. Add green chilies, taco seasoning mix, soup and rice; mix well. Spoon mixture into 8x12-inch baking dish. Top with tomatoes, cheese and corn chips. Bake at 350 degrees for 30 to 35 minutes, or until golden brown.

Approx Per Serving: Cal 497; Prot 28 g; Carbo 38 g; Fiber 2 g; T Fat 26 g; Chol 89 mg; Sod 1490 mg.

Enchilada Pie

Yield: 8 servings Utensil: baking dish Preheat: 350 degrees

2 pounds ground beef
1 onion, chopped
1 green bell pepper, chopped
1 4-ounce can chopped green chilies
1 envelope taco seasoning mix
2 8-ounce cans tomato sauce
4 6-inch flour tortillas
½ cup sliced olives
2 cups shredded Cheddar cheese

Brown ground beef with onion and green pepper in skillet, stirring until ground beef is crumbly; drain. Add green chilies, taco seasoning and tomato sauce; mix well. Simmer for 15 minutes, stirring occasionally. Place 2 tortillas in bottom of greased 8x12-inch baking dish. Layer with half the sauce, half the olives and half the cheese. Repeat layers. Bake, covered with aluminum foil, at 350 degrees for 30 minutes. Let stand for 5 to 10 minutes or until cool. Cut into squares to serve.

Approx Per Serving: Cal 480; Prot 32 g; Carbo 24 g; Fiber 4 g; T Fat 30 g; Chol 104 mg; Sod 1182 mg.

Ground Beef Upside-Down Corn Bread

Yield: 6 servings   Utensil: baking dish   Preheat: 400 degrees

1 cup chopped onion
2 tablespoons margarine
1½ pounds ground chuck
1 teaspoon chili powder
⅛ teaspoon pepper
1 teaspoon salt
¼ cup chopped black olives
1 10-ounce can tomato paste
1 tablespoon flour
1 tablespoon water
1 12-ounce package corn bread mix
1 tablespoon chopped parsley

Sauté onion in margarine in skillet. Add ground chuck, stirring until crumbly; drain. Add chili powder, pepper, salt, olives and tomato paste; mix well. Blend flour with 1 tablespoon water in bowl. Add gradually to ground chuck mixture, stirring constantly. Cook until sauce is thickened, stirring constantly. Spread evenly in 9x9-inch baking dish. Prepare corn bread batter using package directions. Spoon over ground beef mixture. Bake at 400 degrees for 20 minutes. Invert onto serving plate. Garnish with parsley.

Approx Per Serving: Cal 478; Prot 26 g; Carbo 34 g; Fiber 4 g; T Fat 28 g; Chol 116 mg; Sod 859 mg.

Barbecued Meatballs

Yield: 6 servings   Utensil: electric skillet   Preheat: 360 degrees

1½ pounds ground beef
¾ cup oats
1 tablespoon minced onion
1½ teaspoons salt
¼ teaspoon pepper
1 cup milk
½ cup flour
3 tablespoons shortening
2 tablespoons sugar
2 tablespoons Worcestershire sauce
1 cup catsup
½ cup water
¼ cup vinegar
½ cup minced onion

Combine ground beef, oats, 1 tablespoon minced onion, salt, pepper and milk in bowl; mix well. Shape mixture into 18 balls. Coat with flour. Brown in oil in electric skillet at 360 degrees; drain. Combine sugar, Worcestershire sauce, catsup, water, vinegar and ½ cup minced onion in small bowl; mix well. Pour over meatballs. Simmer, covered, at 200 to 220 degrees for 1½ hours or until desired degree of doneness.

Approx Per Serving: Cal 463; Prot 26 g; Carbo 35 g; Fiber 2 g; T Fat 25 g; Chol 80 mg; Sod 1139 mg.

Oven Porcupines

Yield: 6 servings   Utensil: baking dish   Preheat: 350 degrees

1 pound ground beef
½ cup uncooked rice
½ cup water
⅓ cup chopped onion
1 teaspoon salt
½ teaspoon celery salt
⅛ teaspoon garlic powder
⅛ teaspoon pepper
⅛ teaspoon garlic powder
1 15-ounce can tomato sauce
1 15-ounce can water
2 teaspoons Worcestershire sauce

Combine ground beef, rice, water, onion, salt, celery salt, ⅛ teaspoon garlic powder and pepper in large bowl; mix well. Shape mixture into balls. Arrange in ungreased 8x8-inch baking dish. Combine remaining ⅛ teaspoon garlic powder, tomato sauce, water and Worcestershire sauce in small bowl; mix well. Pour over meatballs. Bake, covered with aluminum foil, at 350 degrees for 45 minutes. Remove foil; bake for 15 minutes longer.

Approx Per Serving: Cal 235; Prot 16 g; Carbo 19 g; Fiber 1 g; T Fat 11 g; Chol 49 mg; Sod 1022 mg.

Meat Loaf

Yield: 8 servings   Utensil: loaf pan   Preheat: 350 degrees

1 egg, beaten
½ cup sour cream
½ cup tomato juice
1 teaspoon salt
¼ teaspoon pepper
1½ teaspoons prepared mustard
1 cup bread crumbs
1 pound ground beef
½ pound ground pork
2 wieners, ground
¼ cup chopped onion

Combine egg, sour cream, tomato juice, salt, pepper and mustard in large bowl; mix well. Reserve 2 tablespoons bread crumbs for topping; stir remaining bread crumbs into mixture. Add beef, pork, wieners and onion; mix well. Form mixture into loaf; place in loaf pan. Sprinkle with reserved 2 tablespoons bread crumbs. Bake at 350 degrees for 1 hour; drain. Place on serving platter.

Approx Per Serving: Cal 276; Prot 18 g; Carbo 11 g; Fiber 1 g; T Fat 18 g; Chol 86 mg; Sod 628 mg.

Spaghetti with Meat Sauce

Yield: 4 servings	Utensil: skillet	Preheat: no

1 pound lean ground beef
1/2 cup chopped onion
1 teaspoon garlic salt
1 4-ounce can mushroom pieces, drained
1/4 cup chopped fresh parsley
1 8-ounce can tomato sauce
1 16-ounce can tomatoes
1 teaspoon salt
1/2 teaspoon oregano
1/4 teaspoon pepper
Dash of basil
1 bay leaf
8 ounces uncooked thin spaghetti

Brown ground beef, onion and garlic salt in large skillet, stirring until ground beef is crumbly; drain. Add mushroom pieces, parsley, tomato sauce, tomatoes, salt, oregano, pepper, basil and bay leaf. Simmer, covered, for 1 hour. Simmer, uncovered, for 30 minutes longer or until sauce is of desired consistency. Remove bay leaf. Cook spaghetti using package directions; drain. Spoon meat sauce over spaghetti on platter or individual plates. May substitute 2 teaspoons dried parsley for 1/4 cup fresh parsley.

Approx Per Serving: Cal 490; Prot 31 g; Carbo 60 g; Fiber 7 g; T Fat 11 g; Chol 74 mg; Sod 1940 mg.

Veal Meatballs

Yield: 8 servings	Utensil: baking dish	Preheat: 350 degrees

1 3/4 pounds ground veal
1 cup skim milk
1/2 cup egg substitute
1 1/2 cups bread crumbs
1/2 teaspoon white pepper
1 teaspoon dried parsley flakes
1/4 cup minced onion
1/2 cup grated Parmesan cheese

Combine veal, milk, egg substitute and bread crumbs in large bowl; mix well. Stir in white pepper, parsley, onion and Parmesan cheese. Shape mixture into 1-inch balls. Arrange in 9x13-inch baking dish. Bake at 350 degrees for 15 minutes; drain. May freeze until ready to use. Serve with favorite sauce.

Approx Per Serving: Cal 256; Prot 32 g; Carbo 16 g; Fiber 1 g; T Fat 6 g; Chol 107 mg; Sod 339 mg.

New Orleans Red Beans and Rice

Yield: 8 servings Utensil: saucepan Preheat: no

1 pound dried red beans
1 ham hock
6 stalks celery, chopped
2 green bell peppers, chopped
3 bay leaves
4 cloves of garlic, minced
1 onion, chopped
Dash of Tabasco sauce
1 teaspoon salt
1 teaspoon pepper
2 quarts water
1½ pounds smoked sausage

Soak beans in water to cover in bowl overnight; drain. Combine ham hock, celery, green peppers, bay leaves, garlic, onion, Tabasco sauce, salt and pepper with 2 quarts water in 5-quart saucepan. Simmer for 1 hour, stirring occasionally. Add beans. Simmer for 2 hours longer or until mixture thickens. Slice sausage into ½-inch slices. Add to beans 30 minutes before serving. Remove bay leaves. Serve over rice with salad and French bread.

Approx Per Serving: Cal 377; Prot 19 g; Carbo 39 g; Fiber 14 g; T Fat 17 g; Chol 28 mg; Sod 576 mg.

Burgundy Ham with Green Grapes

Yield: 6 servings Utensil: skillet Preheat: no

1 tablespoon margarine
2 tablespoons sugar
Dash of ginger
6 1½-inch thick ham slices
¾ cup Burgundy
1 tablespoon cornstarch
¼ cup cold water
1 cup seedless green grapes

Melt margarine in large heavy skillet. Sprinkle with sugar and ginger. Brown ham quickly on both sides in sugar mixture; remove from skillet. Stir in wine. Bring to a boil. Blend cornstarch with water in small bowl. Add to sugar mixture gradually, stirring until blended. Simmer until mixture thickens, stirring constantly. Return ham to skillet. Cook, covered, over low heat for 15 minutes. Add grapes. Cook for 1 to 2 minutes longer. Remove ham to warmed serving platter. Spoon grapes and sauce over ham to serve. May substitute Port for Burgundy.

Approx Per Serving: Cal 244; Prot 27 g; Carbo 11 g; Fiber <1 g; T Fat 8 g; Chol 58 mg; Sod 1429 mg.

HAM AND CHICKEN CASSEROLE

Yield: 6 servings   Utensil: casserole   Preheat: 350 degrees

1/2 pound cooked ham, cubed
2 tablespoons finely chopped onion
1 10-ounce can cream of chicken soup
1/2 cup milk
1 tablespoon sugar
1 cup chopped cooked chicken
1 cup cubed American cheese
3 cups soft bread crumbs
1 tablespoon chopped pimento
2 tablespoons melted butter

Brown ham and onion in skillet; set aside. Combine soup and milk in saucepan. Simmer until heated through, stirring to blend. Add sugar, chicken and cheese; mix well. Line bottom of 2-quart casserole with 1 cup bread crumbs. Spread ham and onion mixture over bread crumbs. Sprinkle with 1 cup bread crumbs. Pour chicken mixture over bread crumbs. Sprinkle with remaining 1 cup bread crumbs and pimento. Drizzle with melted butter. Bake at 350 degrees for 30 minutes.

Approx Per Serving: Cal 326; Prot 23 g; Carbo 18 g; Fiber 1 g; T Fat 18 g; Chol 73 mg; Sod 1316 mg.

SWEDISH HAM BALLS

Yield: 10 servings   Utensil: baking dish   Preheat: 275 degrees

1 pound ground ham
1 pound lean ground pork
1/2 pound ground beef
2 cups bread crumbs
2 eggs, beaten
1 cup milk
1 1/2 cups packed brown sugar
1/2 cup water
1/4 cup vinegar
1 teaspoon dry mustard

Combine ham, pork, ground beef, bread crumbs, eggs and milk in large bowl; mix well. Form mixture into balls. Arrange in 9x13-inch baking dish. Combine brown sugar, water, vinegar and mustard in small bowl; stir until blended. Pour sauce over ham balls. Bake at 275 degrees for 2 hours, turning once.

Approx Per Serving: Cal 359; Prot 25 g; Carbo 27 g; Fiber 1 g; T Fat 11 g; Chol 119 mg; Sod 588 mg.

Ham Rolls

Yield: 10 servings   Utensil: 2 baking dishes   Preheat: 350 degrees

1¼ pounds ground ham
1 pound lean ground pork
½ pound ground beef
1½ cups graham cracker crumbs
1 cup milk
2 eggs, beaten
1 10-ounce can tomato soup
½ cup packed brown sugar
2 tablespoons vinegar
1 teaspoon dry mustard

Combine ham, pork, beef, graham cracker crumbs, milk and eggs in large bowl; mix well. Shape mixture into 2-inch balls. Arrange in two 9x13-inch baking dishes. Mix tomato soup, brown sugar, vinegar and dry mustard in bowl, stirring to blend. Pour over ham balls. Bake at 350 degrees for 1 hour.

Approx Per Serving: Cal 336; Prot 26 g; Carbo 30 g; Fiber 1 g; T Fat 12 g; Chol 108 mg; Sod 853 mg.

Ham and Wild Rice Casserole

Yield: 12 servings   Utensil: baking dish   Preheat: 350 degrees

1½ 7-ounce packages long grain and wild rice mix
1 10-ounce package frozen chopped broccoli
1 pound cooked ham, cubed
1 4-ounce can mushrooms, drained, chopped
1 cup cubed sharp Cheddar cheese
1 10-ounce can cream of celery soup
1 cup mayonnaise
2 teaspoons prepared mustard
1 teaspoon curry powder
1¼ cups Parmesan cheese

Cook rice using package directions; drain. Spoon into buttered 9x13-inch baking dish. Cook broccoli using package directions; drain. Layer broccoli, ham, mushrooms and cheese over rice. Blend soup, mayonnaise, mustard and curry powder together in small bowl. Spread over top layer. Sprinkle with Parmesan cheese. Bake at 350 degrees for 45 minutes. Let stand for 5 to 10 minutes or until set before serving.

Approx Per Serving: Cal 381; Prot 16 g; Carbo 24 g; Fiber 1 g; T Fat 22 g; Chol 51 mg; Sod 1070 mg.

Italian Chef's Prime

Yield: 6 servings Utensil: roasting pan Preheat: 325 degrees

3 tablespoons dillseed
1 tablespoon fennel seed
¼ teaspoon oregano
1 teaspoon lemon pepper
¼ teaspoon onion powder
1 4-pound boneless pork roast (Chef's prime)

Combine dillseed, fennel seed, oregano, lemon pepper and onion powder in small bowl; mix well. Coat roast with seasoning mixture. Place in shallow roasting pan. Roast at 325 degrees for 1 to 1½ hours or until temperature registers 155 degrees on meat thermometer. Let roast stand for 5 minutes before slicing.

Approx Per Serving: Cal 436; Prot 60 g; Carbo 0 g; Fiber 0 g; T Fat 20 g; Chol 186 mg; Sod 147 mg.

Pork Loin with Special Sauce

Yield: 12 servings Utensil: microwave-safe rack MW

½ teaspoon salt
½ teaspoon garlic powder
1 teaspoon chili powder
1 4-pound boneless pork loin roast
½ cup catsup
½ cup apple jelly
1 tablespoon vinegar
½ teaspoon chili powder

Combine salt, garlic powder and 1 teaspoon chili powder in shallow bowl; mix well. Roll roast in seasonings. Place on microwave-safe meat rack. Cover top of roast loosely with plastic wrap. Microwave on Medium for 1 hour and 40 minutes or until meat thermometer registers 170 degrees. Let stand for 10 to 15 minutes before slicing. Combine catsup, apple jelly, vinegar and remaining ½ teaspoon chili powder in saucepan; mix well. Simmer until heated through. Spoon sauce over sliced roast.

Approx Per Serving: Cal 263; Prot 30 g; Carbo 11 g; Fiber <1 g; T Fat 10 g; Chol 93 mg; Sod 284 mg.

BAKED IOWA CHOPS

Yield: 6 servings   Utensil: baking pan   Preheat: 350 degrees

1 12-ounce can beer
3 tablespoons light brown sugar
¾ cup catsup
6 Iowa pork chops, trimmed

Combine beer, sugar and catsup in small bowl; mix well. Arrange chops in 9x13-inch baking pan. Pour sauce over chops. Bake at 350 degrees for 1½ hours or until cooked through. May cook in slow cooker for 2½ to 3 hours, if preferred.

Approx Per Serving: Cal 314; Prot 33 g; Carbo 17 g; Fiber 1 g; T Fat 11 g; Chol 98 mg; Sod 439 mg.

MARINATED IOWA CHOPS

Yield: 4 servings   Utensil: gas grill   Preheat: yes

4 Iowa pork chops, trimmed
¼ cup soy sauce
¼ teaspoon thyme
¼ cup chopped onion
½ cup olive oil
⅛ teaspoon pepper
¼ teaspoon dried basil
¼ cup vinegar

Place chops in shallow glass dish. Combine soy sauce, thyme, onion, oil, pepper, basil and vinegar in small bowl; mix well. Pour over chops. Marinate, covered, in refrigerator overnight. Cook over medium heat on gas grill for 30 to 45 minutes or until cooked through.

Approx Per Serving: Cal 482; Prot 33 g; Carbo 3 g; Fiber <1 g; T Fat 37 g; Chol 98 mg; Sod 1106 mg.

PORK CHOPS AND RICE

Yield: 8 servings   Utensil: casserole   Preheat: 325 degrees

8 pork chops, trimmed
1 cup minute rice
1 10-ounce can cream of chicken soup
1 cup milk
Salt and pepper to taste

Brown pork chops on both sides in heavy skillet; drain. Combine rice, chicken soup, milk, salt and pepper to taste in bowl; mix well. Spoon into 9x13-inch casserole. Arrange pork chops on top. Bake at 325 degrees for 1 hour and 15 minutes or until cooked through.

Approx Per Serving: Cal 327; Prot 35 g; Carbo 14 g; Fiber <1 g; T Fat 14 g; Chol 105 mg; Sod 389 mg.

Bacon-Wrapped Pork Loaves

Yield: 8 servings   Utensil: baking dish   Preheat: 350 degrees

2 pounds ground pork
1 egg, beaten
3 tablespoons minced onion
¾ cup grated carrots
¾ cup grated Parmesan cheese
2 teaspoons Worcestershire sauce
3 tablespoons melted butter
1 teaspoon salt
¼ teaspoon pepper
¾ teaspoon celery powder
¾ cup dry bread crumbs
1 cup barbecue sauce
8 slices bacon

Combine pork, egg, onion, carrots, cheese, Worcestershire sauce and butter in large bowl; mix well. Stir in salt, pepper, celery powder and bread crumbs. Shape mixture into 8 loaves. Wrap each loaf with 1 slice bacon, securing bacon with toothpick. Arrange in 9x13-inch baking dish. Bake at 350 degrees for 40 minutes, basting occasionally with barbecue sauce. May cook on barbecue grill for 20 to 30 minutes or until done to taste.

Approx Per Serving: Cal 344; Prot 30 g; Carbo 12 g; Fiber 1 g; T Fat 19 g; Chol 119 mg; Sod 948 mg.

Breakfast Bake

Yield: 8 servings   Utensil: baking pan   Preheat: 300 degrees

1½ cups herb-seasoned croutons
1 cup plain croutons
1½ cups shredded sharp Cheddar cheese
1½ pounds sausage
4 eggs
2¼ cups milk
½ teaspoon salt
Dash of pepper
¾ teaspoon dry mustard
1 10-ounce can cream of mushroom soup
½ soup can milk
1 16-ounce package frozen hashed brown potatoes, thawed
½ cup shredded sharp Cheddar cheese

Sprinkle croutons and 1½ cups cheese in 8x12-inch baking pan. Cook sausage in skillet until brown and crumbly; drain. Spoon cooked sausage over croutons and cheese. Beat eggs and 2¼ cups milk in bowl. Add salt, pepper and mustard; mix well. Pour over sausage. Chill, covered, in refrigerator overnight. Blend soup with ½ soup can milk in bowl. Pour over layers. Sprinkle with potatoes and remaining ½ cup cheese. Bake at 300 degrees for 1½ hours. Serve hot.

Approx Per Serving: Cal 569; Prot 21 g; Carbo 31 g; Fiber 1 g; T Fat 41 g; Chol 176 mg; Sod 1096 mg.

Fancy Egg Scramble

Yield: 8 servings	Utensil: casserole	Preheat: 350 degrees

2 tablespoons margarine
2 tablespoons flour
1/2 teaspoon salt
1/4 teaspoon pepper
2 cups milk
1 cup shredded American cheese
1 cup chopped Canadian bacon
1/4 cup chopped green onions
3 tablespoons margarine
12 eggs, beaten
1 3-ounce can mushrooms, drained
4 teaspoons margarine, melted
2 1/4 cups soft bread crumbs
1/8 teaspoon paprika

Melt 2 tablespoons margarine in saucepan. Stir in flour until blended. Add salt, pepper and milk. Simmer until mixture thickens and bubbles, stirring constantly. Add cheese. Simmer until cheese melts; set aside. Brown Canadian bacon and green onions in 3 tablespoons margarine in skillet, stirring until onions are tender. Add eggs. Scramble until partially set. Stir in mushrooms. Fold in cheese sauce. Coat 7x12-inch casserole with nonstick cooking spray. Pour in egg mixture. Combine melted margarine with bread crumbs and paprika; mix well. Sprinkle over eggs. Chill, covered, for 30 minutes to overnight. Bake, uncovered, at 350 degrees for 30 minutes.

Approx Per Serving: Cal 350; Prot 18 g; Carbo 13 g; Fiber 1 g; T Fat 25 g; Chol 346 mg; Sod 817 mg.

Fettucini

Yield: 6 servings	Utensil: skillet	Preheat: no

16 ounces uncooked fettucini
1 teaspoon salt
1/2 cup butter
1 1/2 packages frozen chopped spinach, thawed, drained
1 pound bacon, crisp-fried, crumbled
1 egg, slightly beaten
2 cups half and half
1 1/2 cups grated Parmesan cheese
1/4 teaspoon pepper
2 teaspoons salt

Cook pasta using package directions using 1 teaspoon salt; drain. Melt butter in large saucepan. Add spinach and bacon. Cook for 5 minutes, stirring constantly. Add noodles; toss lightly with spinach mixture. Beat egg and half and half in small bowl. Add to noodles. Stir in Parmesan cheese, pepper and remaining 2 teaspoons salt. Toss to coat well. Cook, covered, over low heat for 5 minutes or until heated through.

Approx Per Serving: Cal 775; Prot 31 g; Carbo 65 g; Fiber 5 g; T Fat 44 g; Chol 141 mg; Sod 2040 mg.

LASAGNA

Yield: 10 servings   Utensil: baking dish   Preheat: 375 degrees

1½ pounds Italian sausage
1 clove of garlic, minced
1 tablespoon dried basil
1½ teaspoons salt
1   12-ounce can tomato paste
1   15-ounce can tomato sauce
1 cup water
3 pounds ricotta cheese
½ cup grated Parmesan cheese
2 tablespoons dried parsley flakes
3 eggs, beaten
1 teaspoon salt
½ teaspoon pepper
1 cup water
10 ounces uncooked lasagna noodles
1½ pounds mozzarella cheese, thinly sliced

Brown sausage in skillet; drain. Add garlic, basil, salt, tomato paste, tomato sauce and 1 cup water. Simmer for 30 minutes, stirring occasionally. Combine ricotta cheese, Parmesan cheese, parsley, eggs, salt, pepper and remaining 1 cup water in bowl; mix well. Cook noodles using package directions; drain. Place ½ of the noodles in 9x13-inch baking dish. Layer ½ of the cheese mixture, ½ of the sliced mozzarella cheese and ½ of the meat sauce over noodles. Repeat layers. Bake, covered, at 375 degrees for 35 minutes. Bake, uncovered, for 25 minutes longer. Let stand for 10 minutes. Cut into squares to serve. May substitute Romano cheese for Parmesan cheese.

Approx Per Serving: Cal 722; Prot 44 g; Carbo 37 g; Fiber 2 g; T Fat 44 g; Chol 213 mg; Sod 1575 mg.

ASPARAGUS QUICHE

Yield: 6 servings   Utensil: pie plate   Preheat: 450 degrees

1   9-inch pie shell
4 eggs, slightly beaten
½ cup milk
1 cup whipping cream
1 cup shredded Cheddar cheese
1 small onion, thinly sliced
½ teaspoon nutmeg
½ teaspoon sage
½ teaspoon pepper
2 teaspoons salt
1 cup chopped fresh asparagus

Bake pie shell at 450 degrees for 7 minutes. Combine eggs, milk, whipping cream, cheese and onion in bowl; mix well. Stir in nutmeg, sage, pepper and salt. Line pie crust with asparagus pieces. Pour egg mixture over asparagus. Bake at 350 degrees for 45 minutes or until golden brown. Let stand to cool; cut into wedges to serve.

Approx Per Serving: Cal 440; Prot 13 g; Carbo 18 g; Fiber 1 g; T Fat 35 g; Chol 219 mg; Sod 1081 mg.

Egg-Asparagus Burritos

Yield: 4 servings   Utensil: skillet   Preheat: 350 degrees

24 fresh asparagus spears
1½ teaspoons lemon juice
5 eggs, beaten
⅓ cup skim milk
1½ tablespoons chopped green onions
¼ teaspoon salt
½ teaspoon pepper
8 6-inch flour tortillas
¾ cup shredded Monterey Jack cheese

Trim asparagus stems. Steam in vegetable steamer or in microwave until tender-crisp. Toss with lemon juice; set aside. Combine eggs, milk, 1½ tablespoons green onions, salt and pepper in bowl; mix well. Coat skillet with nonstick cooking spray. Add egg mixture. Scramble until partially set. Place damp paper towel between tortillas; wrap in aluminum foil. Bake at 350 degrees for 5 to 10 minutes or until softened. Place 3 asparagus spears in center of each tortilla. Top each with ⅛ of the egg mixture and 1½ tablespoons cheese. Roll up. Place seam side down on serving plates. Garnish with warmed salsa, sour cream and additional green onions.

Approx Per Serving: Cal 381; Prot 22 g; Carbo 39 g; Fiber 7 g; T Fat 17 g; Chol 286 mg; Sod 520 mg.

Easy Blintz Brunch

Yield: 8 servings   Utensil: baking dish   Preheat: 350 degrees

¼ cup melted butter
12 frozen cheese blintzes, thawed
4 eggs, beaten
½ cup sugar
¼ teaspoon salt
1½ cups sour cream
¼ cup frozen orange juice concentrate
1 teaspoon vanilla extract
1 teaspoon almond extract

Pour melted butter into 9x13-inch glass baking dish. Arrange frozen blintzes in prepared dish. Combine eggs, sugar, salt, sour cream, orange juice concentrate, vanilla and almond extracts in bowl; mix well. Pour over blintzes. May store covered in refrigerator at this point until ready to use. Bake at 350 degrees for 35 to 40 minutes or until sauce is bubbly.

Approx Per Serving: Cal 244; Prot 5 g; Carbo 18 g; Fiber <1 g; T Fat 18 g; Chol 141 mg; Sod 173 mg.
Nutritional information does not include cheese blintzes.

Meatless Lasagna

Yield: 12 servings   Utensil: baking dish   Preheat: 375 degrees

1/2 cup chopped onion
1 teaspoon minced garlic
1 8-ounce jar mushrooms, drained, chopped
2 tablespoons olive oil
2 1/2 cups prepared spaghetti sauce
8 ounces uncooked lasagna noodles
1 16-ounce can pinto beans, drained, mashed
3 cups non-fat cottage cheese, drained
1 cup mozzarella cheese, sliced
1/4 cup grated Parmesan cheese

Sauté onion, garlic and mushrooms in oil in skillet. Stir in prepared spaghetti sauce. Simmer for 5 minutes or until heated through, stirring frequently. Cook noodles using package directions; drain. Layer 1/2 of the noodles, 1/2 of the spaghetti sauce, 1/2 of the pinto beans, 1/2 of the cottage cheese, and 1/2 of the mozzarella cheese in 9x13-inch baking dish. Repeat layers. Sprinkle with Parmesan cheese. Bake at 375 degrees for 1 hour. Let stand for a few minutes to set. Cut into squares to serve.

Approx Per Serving: Cal 279; Prot 17 g; Carbo 35 g; Fiber 5 g; T Fat 8 g; Chol 9 mg; Sod 565 mg.

Quesadillas

Yield: 6 servings   Utensil: griddle   Preheat: yes

12 ounces Monterey Jack cheese, shredded
1 4-ounce jar jalapeño peppers, drained, chopped
12 6-inch flour tortillas

Place 2 tablespoons cheese and 2 teaspoons jalapeño peppers on each tortilla. Fold over to enclose filling. Brown on griddle until cheese melts. Serve hot with salsa.

Approx Per Serving: Cal 374; Prot 18 g; Carbo 30 g; Fiber 2 g; T Fat 21 g; Chol 52 mg; Sod 781 mg.

Poultry and Seafood Main Dishes

Perfect Roasted Chicken

Yield: 8 servings   Utensil: roasting pan   Preheat: 475 degrees

2 roasting chickens
2 teaspoons butter, softened
1 teaspoon thyme
2 stalks celery, chopped
2 onions
4 teaspoons butter, melted
Salt to taste
6 carrots, thickly sliced

Rinse chicken; pat dry. Place 1 teaspoon butter, 1/2 teaspoon thyme, half the chopped celery and 1 onion in cavity of each chicken. Brush outsides with 2 teaspoons butter; salt inside and out. Add enough water to roasting pan to cover bottom of pan. Add carrots. Place chickens breast side down on rack in roasting pan. Bake at 475 degrees for 10 minutes. Reduce temperature to 450 degrees. Bake for 20 minutes. Turn breast side up. Bake for 15 minutes. Reduce temperature to 350 degrees. Roast for 30 minutes or until crisp and brown.

Approx Per Serving: Cal 279; Prot 34 g; Carbo 9 g; Fiber 3 g; T Fat 12 g; Chol 109 mg; Sod 150 mg.

Chicken Broccoli Casserole

Yield: 8 servings   Utensil: baking pan   Preheat: 325 degrees

2 4 1/2-ounce packages creamy chicken-rice mix with sauce
1 10-ounce package frozen chopped broccoli, thawed
2 cups chopped cooked chicken
1 4-ounce can sliced mushrooms, drained
1 cup shredded sharp Cheddar cheese
1 10-ounce can cream of celery soup
1 cup light mayonnaise
2 teaspoons prepared mustard
1 teaspoon curry powder
1/4 cup grated Parmesan cheese

Cook rice using package instructions. Spread in 9x13-inch baking pan. Place broccoli over rice. Combine chicken, mushrooms and cheese in bowl. Spoon over broccoli. Blend soup, mayonnaise, mustard and curry powder together in small bowl. Pour over chicken layer. Sprinkle Parmesan cheese over top layer. Bake at 325 degrees for 45 minutes. May substitute canned chicken, chopped cooked ham or chopped cooked turkey for chicken.

Approx Per Serving: Cal 234; Prot 15 g; Carbo 10 g; Fiber 1 g; T Fat 15 g; Chol 54 mg; Sod 682 mg.
Nutritional information does not include chicken-rice mix.

CHICKEN DIVINE

Yield: 12 servings   Utensil: casserole   Preheat: 350 degrees

6 chicken breasts, cooked, chopped
2 10-ounce cans cream of mushroom soup
1½ cups chopped celery
1 cup mayonnaise
¼ cup white wine
2 8-ounce cans water chestnuts, drained, sliced
1 8-ounce package corn bread stuffing mix
½ cup butter, melted

Combine chopped chicken, soup, celery, mayonnaise and wine in bowl; mix well. Layer chicken mixture and water chestnuts in greased 9x13-inch casserole. Sprinkle with stuffing mix. Drizzle with melted butter. Bake at 350 degrees for 35 to 45 minutes or until golden brown.

Approx Per Serving: Cal 396; Prot 22 g; Carbo 14 g; Fiber 1 g; T Fat 28 g; Chol 81 mg; Sod 744 mg.

ELEGANT CHICKEN

Yield: 4 servings   Utensil: skillet   Preheat: no

2 whole chicken breasts, boned, skinned
¼ cup flour
2 tablespoons butter
2 tablespoons vegetable oil
¾ cup orange juice
¼ cup dry white wine
1 cup fresh mushrooms, sliced
2 tablespoons chopped parsley
½ teaspoon dried rosemary
1 orange, peeled, sectioned
1 avocado, sliced lengthwise

Rinse chicken breasts; pat dry. Place between 2 sheets of waxed paper; pound to flatten. Coat with flour. Melt butter and oil in skillet. Brown chicken breasts on both sides. Add orange juice, wine, mushrooms, parsley and rosemary; mix well. Simmer for 5 minutes or until chicken is tender. Remove chicken breasts to heated serving platter. Bring sauce to a boil. Cook until slightly thickened, stirring constantly. Pour over chicken. Garnish with orange sections and avocado slices.

Approx Per Serving: Cal 363; Prot 23 g; Carbo 19 g; Fiber 6 g; T Fat 22 g; Chol 65 mg; Sod 112 mg.

Chicken Enchilada Bake

Yield: 6 servings   Utensil: microwave-safe casserole   MW

½ cup chopped onion
1 tablespoon margarine
1 10-ounce can cream of chicken soup
1 cup sour cream
¼ teaspoon ground coriander
¼ teaspoon ground cumin
12 corn tortillas, torn into bite-sized pieces
3 cups cubed cooked chicken
1 4-ounce can chopped green chilies, drained
8 ounces shredded Cheddar cheese
8 ounces shredded Monterey Jack cheese

Place onion and margarine in microwave-safe dish. Microwave, covered, on High for 2 to 4 minutes. Stir in soup, sour cream, coriander and cumin. Layer ½ of the tortilla pieces, ½ of the chicken, ½ of the chilies, ½ of the soup mixture and ½ of the Cheddar and Monterey Jack cheeses in a 2-quart microwave-safe casserole. Repeat layers, omitting cheeses. Cover loosely with plastic wrap. Microwave on High for 9 to 12 minutes or until bubbly. Sprinkle remaining cheeses on top; cover. Let stand for 5 minutes before serving.

Approx Per Serving: Cal 715; Prot 46 g; Carbo 35 g; Fiber 5 g; T Fat 44 g; Chol 158 mg; Sod 942 mg.

Scalloped Chicken

Yield: 10 servings   Utensil: baking dish   Preheat: 350 degrees

4 cups cubed cooked chicken
6 cups dried bread crumbs
1¼ teaspoons sage
2 tablespoons minced onion
¾ teaspoon salt
¾ teaspoon pepper
4 cups chicken broth
¼ cup flour

Place cubed chicken in 9x13-inch baking dish. Combine bread crumbs, sage, onion, salt and pepper in bowl; mix well. Sprinkle over chicken. Blend chicken broth and flour in small bowl. Pour over bread crumbs. Bake at 350 degrees for 1 hour.

Approx Per Serving: Cal 341; Prot 23 g; Carbo 47 g; Fiber 3 g; T Fat 7 g; Chol 41 mg; Sod 944 mg.

CHICKEN-MACARONI CASSEROLE

Yield: 10 servings	Utensil: baking dish	Preheat: 375 degrees

4 cups chopped cooked chicken
2 cups uncooked macaroni
8 ounces Velveeta cheese, cubed
1 onion, chopped
4 hard-boiled eggs, chopped
2 10-ounce cans cream of mushroom soup
2 cups chicken broth

Combine chopped chicken, uncooked macaroni, cheese, onion, eggs, soup and chicken broth in large bowl; mix well. Spoon mixture into greased 10x14-inch baking dish. May store in refrigerator overnight at this point. Bake at 375 degrees for 1 hour. Serve hot.

Approx Per Serving: Cal 317; Prot 19 g; Carbo 23 g; Fiber 1 g; T Fat 16 g; Chol 128 mg; Sod 1021 mg.

CHICKEN AND RICE CASSEROLE

Yield: 6 servings	Utensil: baking pan	Preheat: 300 degrees

1 cup uncooked brown rice
1 10-ounce can cream of chicken soup
1 10-ounce can cream of celery soup
3/4 cup milk
1 3-pound chicken, skinned, cut into serving pieces
1 envelope onion soup mix

Pour rice into well greased 9x13-inch baking pan. Blend chicken soup, celery soup and milk in small bowl. Pour over rice. Rinse chicken; pat dry. Arrange over soup and rice. Sprinkle with onion soup mix. Bake, covered with foil, at 300 degrees for 2½ to 3 hours or until chicken is tender.

Approx Per Serving: Cal 432; Prot 38 g; Carbo 33 g; Fiber 1 g; T Fat 15 g; Chol 115 mg; Sod 1001 mg.

Chicken and Spaghetti Casserole

Yield: 10 servings   Utensil: baking pan   Preheat: 375 degrees

1 3-pound chicken
7 ounces spaghetti, cooked
2 10-ounce cans cream of mushroom soup
8 ounces shredded Velveeta cheese
1 onion, minced
6 hard-boiled eggs, chopped
1 2-ounce jar chopped pimento, drained
1 cup crushed potato chips

Rinse chicken. Place in large saucepan with water to cover. Simmer for 1 hour or until chicken is tender. Drain, reserving 2 cups broth. Let stand to cool. Bone and chop chicken. Combine with cooked spaghetti, soup, cheese, onion, eggs, pimento and reserved chicken broth in large bowl; mix well. Pour into 9x12-inch baking pan. Sprinkle with crushed chips. Bake at 375 degrees for 45 minutes.

Approx Per Serving: Cal 426; Prot 34 g; Carbo 24 g; Fiber 2 g; T Fat 22 g; Chol 212 mg; Sod 1086 mg.

Hot Chicken Salad

Yield: 8 servings   Utensil: casserole   Preheat: 350 degrees

2 cups cubed cooked chicken
2 cups chopped celery
1/2 cup coarsely chopped almonds
1/3 cup chopped green bell pepper
2 tablespoons minced onion
2 tablespoons chopped pimentos
1/2 teaspoon salt
1 cup mayonnaise
2 tablespoons lemon juice
2 cups crushed potato chips
1/3 cup shredded Swiss cheese

Combine chicken, celery, almonds, green pepper and onion together in large bowl; mix well. Stir in pimentos, salt, mayonnaise, lemon juice and 1 1/2 cups crushed chips. Spoon mixture into buttered 2-quart casserole. Sprinkle with remaining 1/2 cup crushed chips and Swiss cheese. Bake at 350 degrees for 20 to 25 minutes or until cheese is melted. Serve with hot rolls and fresh fruit.

Approx Per Serving: Cal 363; Prot 12 g; Carbo 8 g; Fiber 2 g; T Fat 32 g; Chol 46 mg; Sod 387 mg.

Huntington Chicken and Noodles

Yield: 6 servings   Utensil: casserole   Preheat: 350 degrees

¼ cup flour
1 cup half and half
2 cups chicken broth
1 cup shredded Cheddar cheese
2 cups cubed cooked chicken
2 cups cooked noodles
3 to 4 tablespoons chopped pimentos
Salt and pepper to taste

Blend flour with half and half in small bowl. Combine with chicken broth in large saucepan. Simmer until thickened, stirring constantly. Add cheese gradually, stirring until melted. Stir in chicken, noodles, pimentos, salt and pepper to taste. Pour into buttered 2-quart casserole. Bake at 350 degrees for 45 to 60 minutes or until bubbly. May sprinkle with buttered bread crumbs before baking.

Approx Per Serving: Cal 297; Prot 21 g; Carbo 20 g; Fiber 1 g; T Fat 15 g; Chol 69 mg; Sod 425 mg.

Chicken Cordon Bleu

Yield: 6 servings   Utensil: skillet   Preheat: no

6 whole chicken breasts, skinned, boned
1 8-ounce package Swiss cheese slices
1 6-ounce package sliced ham
3 tablespoons flour
1 teaspoon paprika
6 tablespoons butter
1 cup water
1 chicken bouillon cube
1 tablespoon cornstarch
1 cup half and half
5 cups cooked rice

Rinse chicken; pat dry. Flatten on work surface. Place 1 slice cheese and 1 slice ham on one side of each chicken breast. Fold other side over to enclose filling; secure with toothpick. Mix flour and paprika on sheet of waxed paper. Coat chicken in mixture. Melt butter in large skillet. Brown chicken on both sides. Add water and bouillon cube. Bring to a boil, stirring to dissolve bouillon cube. Simmer, covered, for 30 minutes or until chicken is tender. Arrange chicken on warmed serving platter; discard toothpicks. Blend cornstarch and half and half in small bowl. Add to pan drippings. Simmer until thickened, stirring constantly. Serve sauce over chicken and rice.

Approx Per Serving: Cal 733; Prot 62 g; Carbo 49 g; Fiber 1 g; T Fat 30 g; Chol 194 mg; Sod 889 mg.

POULTRY

Chicken Creole

Yield: 4 servings   Utensil: skillet   Preheat: no

4½ tablespoons butter
3 tablespoons flour
3 cloves of garlic, minced
½ cup chopped onion
1 cup chopped green bell pepper
½ cup chopped celery
8 ounces mushrooms, sliced
2 15-ounce cans tomato sauce with tomato bits
Salt and pepper to taste
Hot pepper sauce to taste
½ teaspoon dried basil
4 teaspoons sugar
1½ tablespoons chopped parsley
1½ pounds chopped cooked chicken

Melt butter in large skillet. Stir in flour. Cook over medium heat for 10 minutes, stirring until blended. Add garlic, onion, green pepper, celery and mushrooms. Cook until onion is transparent, stirring occasionally. Add tomato sauce, salt and pepper to taste, hot pepper sauce to taste, basil, sugar and parsley; mix well. Simmer for 15 minutes, stirring frequently, adding water if sauce becomes too thick. Add cooked chicken. Simmer until heated through. Serve over cooked rice. May substitute shrimp for chicken.

Approx Per Serving: Cal 572; Prot 55 g; Carbo 31 g; Fiber 5 g; T Fat 26 g; Chol 187 mg; Sod 1558 mg.

Chicken Cutlets

Yield: 4 servings   Utensil: electric skillet   Preheat: yes

4 chicken breast filets
Salt, pepper and garlic powder to taste
3 eggs, beaten
2 tablespoons milk
1 tablespoon water
1½ cups cracker crumbs
¼ cup grated Parmesan cheese
2 tablespoons chopped parsley
¾ cup vegetable oil

Pound chicken lightly with mallet to flatten. Sprinkle with salt, pepper and garlic powder. Dip in mixture of eggs, milk and water. Roll in mixture of cracker crumbs, Parmesan cheese and parsley. Fry in hot oil in electric skillet for 6 minutes on each side or until tender. Arrange chicken on serving platter.

Approx Per Serving: Cal 673; Prot 28 g; Carbo 24 g; Fiber 1 g; T Fat 51 g; Chol 224 mg; Sod 612 mg.
Nutritional information includes entire amount of oil for frying.

Lemony Chicken

Yield: 4 servings   Utensil: skillet   Preheat: no

2 whole chicken breasts, skinned, split
1 lemon
¼ cup flour
½ teaspoon paprika
2 tablespoons corn oil
2 tablespoons light brown sugar
½ cup chicken broth
1 lemon, thinly sliced

Rinse chicken; pat dry. Grate peel from 1 lemon; set aside. Squeeze lemon juice over chicken breasts. Roll chicken in mixture of flour and paprika. Brown in hot oil in skillet for 5 minutes on each side. Sprinkle chicken with reserved lemon peel and brown sugar. Add chicken broth. Cook, covered, over low heat for 25 minutes. Arrange lemon slices over chicken in skillet. Cook for 10 minutes longer or until chicken is tender. Arrange on serving platter.

Approx Per Serving: Cal 212; Prot 21 g; Carbo 13 g; Fiber <1 g; T Fat 8 g; Chol 49 mg; Sod 155 mg.

Chicken with Orange Sauce

Yield: 4 servings   Utensil: skillet   Preheat: no

½ cup orange juice
⅛ teaspoon dry mustard
⅛ teaspoon garlic salt
3 tablespoons red plum jelly
1 teaspoon minced onion
1 teaspoon margarine
1 tablespoon cornstarch
2 tablespoons orange juice
4 chicken breast filets, cooked

Combine ½ cup orange juice, mustard, garlic salt, jelly, onion and margarine in skillet. Simmer until blended, stirring frequently. Dissolve cornstarch in remaining 2 tablespoons orange juice in bowl. Add to mixture. Cook over medium heat until thickened, stirring constantly. Bring to a boil. Cook for 1 minute, stirring constantly. Pour sauce over cooked chicken breasts.

Approx Per Serving: Cal 162; Prot 20 g; Carbo 15 g; Fiber <1 g; T Fat 2 g; Chol 49 mg; Sod 134 mg.

Chicken Parmigiana

Yield: 6 servings   Utensil: baking dish   Preheat: 350 degrees

3 whole chicken breasts, split, skinned, boned
2 eggs, lightly beaten
1 teaspoon salt
1/8 teaspoon pepper
3/4 cup dry bread crumbs
1/2 cup vegetable oil
2 8-ounce cans tomato sauce
1/4 teaspoon basil
1/8 teaspoon garlic powder
1 tablespoon butter
1/2 cup grated Parmesan cheese
8 ounces mozzarella cheese, sliced, cut into triangles

Rinse chicken; pat dry. Pound to 1/4-inch thickness. Dip in mixture of eggs, salt and pepper. Coat with bread crumbs. Brown chicken breasts on both sides in hot oil in skillet; drain. Remove chicken to 9x13-inch baking dish. Add tomato sauce, basil and garlic powder to skillet. Bring to a boil. Simmer for 10 minutes or until thickened, stirring constantly. Stir in butter. Pour sauce over chicken. Sprinkle with Parmesan cheese. Bake, covered, at 350 degrees for 30 minutes. Arrange slices of mozzarella cheese over chicken. Bake, uncovered, for 10 minutes longer or until cheese melts.

Approx Per Serving: Cal 526; Prot 39 g; Carbo 16 g; Fiber 2 g; T Fat 34 g; Chol 171 mg; Sod 1277 mg.

Sautéed Chicken Breasts in Cream Sauce

Yield: 6 servings   Utensil: skillet   Preheat: no

2 whole chicken breasts, split, skinned, boned
2 tablespoons margarine
1 1/2 cups sliced mushrooms
1 cup chopped celery
1/2 onion, thinly sliced
1/2 teaspoon pepper
1/2 teaspoon dried basil
1/8 teaspoon dried thyme
1/4 cup dry white wine
8 ounces cream cheese, cubed
1/3 cup milk
8 ounces tri-colored corkscrew noodles, cooked

Rinse chicken; pat dry. Cut into strips. Melt margarine in large skillet. Add chicken, mushrooms, celery and onion. Stir in pepper, basil and thyme. Simmer for 10 minutes or until chicken is tender, stirring occasionally. Add 2 tablespoons wine. Simmer for 5 minutes longer. Combine cream cheese, milk and remaining 2 tablespoons wine in saucepan. Simmer, stirring until mixture is smooth. Place cooked noodles on serving platter. Spoon chicken mixture over noodles. Pour cream cheese sauce over all. Garnish with fresh basil leaves.

Approx Per Serving: Cal 394; Prot 22 g; Carbo 33 g; Fiber 2 g; T Fat 19 g; Chol 76 mg; Sod 218 mg.

Chinese Stir-Fry

Yield: 2 servings   Utensil: wok   Preheat: yes

12 ounces chopped uncooked chicken
2 teaspoons vegetable oil
1/2 cup sliced carrots
1/2 cup chopped broccoli
1/2 cup sliced onion
1/2 cup sliced celery
3 tablespoons cornstarch
2 cups water

Rinse chicken; pat dry. Stir-fry in hot oil in wok. Add carrots, broccoli, onion and celery. Stir-fry for 2 to 4 minutes or until vegetables are tender-crisp. Dissolve cornstarch in water. Pour over chicken and vegetables. Simmer until thickened, stirring constantly. Serve over cooked rice.

Approx Per Serving: Cal 307; Prot 30 g; Carbo 34 g; Fiber 7 g; T Fat 6 g; Chol 61 mg; Sod 132 mg.

Stir-Fried Chicken and Vegetables

Yield: 6 servings   Utensil: wok   Preheat: yes

2 whole boneless chicken breasts, cubed
1 tablespoon soy sauce
1 tablespoon cornstarch
2 tablespoons vegetable oil
10 to 12 green onions, chopped
1 8-ounce can sliced water chestnuts, drained
1 8-ounce can sliced mushrooms, drained
1 8-ounce can bamboo shoots, drained
1 tablespoon cornstarch
2 tablespoons soy sauce
1/4 cup chicken broth

Rinse chicken; pat dry. Marinate in mixture of 1 tablespoon soy sauce and 1 tablespoon cornstarch in refrigerator for 1 to 2 hours. Stir-fry chicken in hot oil in wok for 2 to 3 minutes or until done. Remove from wok. Stir-fry green onions for 1 minute. Add water chestnuts, mushrooms and bamboo shoots. Stir-fry for 3 to 5 minutes or until vegetables are tender-crisp. Add chicken back to wok. Dissolve remaining 1 tablespoon cornstarch in remaining 2 tablespoons soy sauce and chicken broth in bowl. Add to wok. Cook until thickened, stirring constantly. Serve over cooked rice.

Approx Per Serving: Cal 162; Prot 16 g; Carbo 13 g; Fiber 3 g; T Fat 5 g; Chol 33 mg; Sod 751 mg.
Nutritional information includes entire amount of marinade.

Chicken Tetrazzini

Yield: 8 servings	Utensil: baking dish	Preheat: 350 degrees

1/2 cup chopped celery
1/2 cup chopped onions
1 green bell pepper, chopped
1/2 cup margarine
1 8-ounce package spaghetti
1 3-pound chicken, cooked, boned, chopped
2 tablespoons chopped jalapeñ peppers
1 2-ounce jar chopped pimentos, drained
1 10-ounce can cream of mushroom soup
1 10-ounce can chicken broth
1 cup grated Parmesan cheese

Sauté celery, onions and green pepper in margarine in skillet. Cook spaghetti using package directions; drain. Combine sautéed vegetables, spaghetti, chicken, jalapeño peppers, pimentos, mushroom soup and chicken broth in large bowl; mix well. Spoon into 9x13-inch greased baking dish. Sprinkle with cheese. Bake at 350 degrees for 30 minutes.

Approx Per Serving: Cal 469; Prot 34 g; Carbo 27 g; Fiber 2 g; T Fat 24 g; Chol 84 mg; Sod 864 mg.

Chicken à la King

Yield: 8 servings	Utensil: saucepan	Preheat: no

1 6-ounce can sliced mushrooms, drained
1/2 cup chopped green bell pepper
1/2 cup butter
1/2 cup flour
1 teaspoon salt
1/4 teaspoon pepper
2 cups chicken broth
2 cups half and half
4 cups chopped cooked chicken
1 4-ounce jar chopped pimentos, drained
8 pastry shells

Sauté mushrooms and green pepper in butter in saucepan, stirring until tender. Remove from heat. Blend in flour, salt and pepper. Cook over low heat until mixture is thickened and bubbly, stirring constantly. Remove from heat. Stir in chicken broth and half and half. Bring to a boil. Cook for 1 minute, stirring constantly. Add chicken and pimentos. Cook until heated through. Spoon into pastry shells on individual serving plates. May substitute turkey for chicken or serve in toast cups if preferred.

Approx Per Serving: Cal 656; Prot 23 g; Carbo 30 g; Fiber 2 g; T Fat 50 g; Chol 146 mg; Sod 988 mg.

CHICKEN IN WINE AND CREAM SAUCE

Yield: 6 servings   Utensil: casserole   Preheat: 350 degrees

4 whole chicken breasts, split, boned
Salt and pepper to taste
6 tablespoons butter
1 onion, coarsely chopped
8 ounces fresh mushrooms, thinly sliced
8 ounces smoked ham, cut into 1/4-inch cubes
2 tablespoons butter
2 tablespoons flour
1 1/2 cups half and half
1/2 cup dry white wine
1 teaspoon prepared mustard
1 tablespoon *fines herbes*
1 teaspoon dried rosemary, crushed
1 teaspoon Worcestershire sauce
8 ounces seedless white grapes

Rinse chicken; pat dry. Sprinkle with salt and pepper. Melt 6 tablespoons butter in large skillet. Brown chicken breasts slowly on both sides. Remove to 9x13-inch casserole. Sauté onion, mushrooms and ham in pan drippings, stirring until onions are golden brown. Spoon over chicken. Melt remaining 2 tablespoons butter in skillet. Add flour, stirring until blended. Remove from heat. Add half and half and wine, whisking until sauce is smooth and thickened. Add mustard, *fines herbes*, rosemary, salt, pepper and Worcestershire sauce; mix well. Pour sauce over chicken. Bake at 350 degrees for 45 to 60 minutes or until bubbly. Add grapes during last 20 minutes of cooking time. Serve with rice or buttered noodles.

Approx Per Serving: Cal 466; Prot 39 g; Carbo 15 g; Fiber 2 g; T Fat 26 g; Chol 150 mg; Sod 751 mg.

MARINATED TURKEY

Yield: 4 servings   Utensil: grill   Preheat: yes

4 4-ounce turkey breast scallops
1/4 cup soy sauce
1/4 cup vegetable oil
1/4 cup sherry
2 tablespoons lemon juice
2 tablespoons minced onion
1/4 teaspoon ginger
1 clove of garlic, minced
Salt and pepper to taste

Rinse turkey; pat dry. Combine soy sauce, oil, sherry, lemon juice, onion, ginger, garlic, salt and pepper in shallow glass bowl; mix well. Add turkey. Marinate in refrigerator for 4 to 5 hours. Drain, reserving marinade. Place turkey scallops on grill over hot coals. Grill for 10 to 15 minutes, turning and basting frequently with reserved marinade.

Approx Per Serving: Cal 310; Prot 25 g; Carbo 3 g; Fiber <1 g; T Fat 20 g; Chol 72 mg; Sod 1097 mg.
Nutritional information includes entire amount of marinade.

Fish with Mustard Sauce

Yield: 6 servings   Utensil: ovenproof serving dish   Preheat: 400 degrees

12 4-ounce fish filets
¼ cup prepared mustard
2 tablespoons prepared
   horseradish
¼ cup white wine
¼ cup lemon juice
2 tablespoons vegetable
   oil
¼ teaspoon pepper
Salt to taste
2 cups herb-seasoned
   bread crumbs

Place fish filets in 9x13-inch ovenproof serving dish. Combine mustard, horseradish, wine, lemon juice, oil, pepper and salt to taste in bowl; mix well. Pour over fish. Bake, covered, at 400 degrees for 20 to 30 minutes or until fish flakes easily. Sprinkle with bread crumbs. Broil for 5 minutes or until lightly browned. Garnish with lemon and orange slices and parsley.

Approx Per Serving: Cal 478; Prot 53 g; Carbo 26 g; Fiber 1 g;
     T Fat 16 g; Chol 116 mg; Sod 521 mg.

Sole Florentine

Yield: 8 servings   Utensil: baking dish   Preheat: 375 degrees

3 10-ounce packages
   frozen chopped
   spinach, thawed
2 cups sour cream
3 tablespoons flour
½ cup finely chopped
   green onions
Juice of 1 lemon
2 teaspoons salt
8 ½-inch thick filets of
   sole
2 tablespoons margarine
Dash of paprika

Cook spinach using package direction; drain well. Mix sour cream, flour, green onions, lemon juice and salt in small bowl. Add half the mixture to spinach. Spread in 9x13-inch baking dish. Arrange fish filets over spinach mixture. Dot with margarine. Spread remaining sour cream mixture over fish. Dust with paprika. Bake at 375 degrees for 30 minutes or until fish flakes easily. May substitute low-fat sour cream and omit margarine to reduce fat content.

Approx Per Serving: Cal 342; Prot 34 g; Carbo 11 g; Fiber 3 g;
     T Fat 18 g; Chol 69 mg; Sod 762 mg.

Yogurt Baked Fish

Yield: 2 servings | Utensil: baking pan | Preheat: 350 degrees

4 medium frozen mahi-mahi filets, thawed
1½ cups piña colada yogurt
½ cup sliced macadamia nuts

Place fish filets in lightly greased 8x8-inch baking pan. Spread yogurt thickly over filets. Sprinkle macadamia nuts over top. Bake at 350 degrees for 20 to 25 minutes or until fish flakes easily.

Approx Per Serving: Cal 858; Prot 84 g; Carbo 17 g; Fiber 2 g; T Fat 50 g; Chol 210 mg; Sod 281 mg.

Fiery Cajun Shrimp

Yield: 10 servings | Utensil: casserole | Preheat: 400 degrees

1 cup melted butter
1 cup melted margarine
½ cup Worcestershire sauce
¼ cup pepper
1 teaspoon rosemary
2 teaspoons Tabasco sauce
2 teaspoons sea salt
3 cloves of garlic, minced
Juice of 2 lemons
6 pounds large fresh unpeeled shrimp
2 lemons, sliced

Combine butter, margarine, Worcestershire sauce, pepper, rosemary, Tabasco sauce, sea salt, garlic and lemon juice in bowl; mix well. Pour ½ cup sauce into 5-quart casserole to cover bottom. Arrange layers of shrimp and lemon slices in casserole. Pour remaining sauce over top. Bake, uncovered, at 400 degrees for 15 to 30 minutes or until shrimp turn pink, stirring occasionally. Serve with crispy French bread, napkins, and plenty of ice water.

Approx Per Serving: Cal 561; Prot 47 g; Carbo 6 g; Fiber 1 g; T Fat 39 g; Chol 474 mg; Sod 1405 mg.

Baked Shrimp Creole

Yield: 8 servings   Utensil: baking pan   Preheat: 350 degrees

½ cup olive oil
¼ cup soy sauce
½ cup margarine, melted
1 tablespoon Italian seasoning
¼ cup lemon juice
4 cloves of garlic, minced
½ cup Sauterne wine
1 tablespoon salt
2 pounds fresh shrimp in shells

Combine oil, soy sauce, margarine, Italian seasoning, lemon juice, garlic, wine and salt in bowl; mix well. Arrange shrimp in 10x15-inch baking pan. Pour sauce over shrimp. Bake at 350 degrees for 30 minutes, stirring occasionally. Serve in deep bowls with French bread and tossed salad.

Approx Per Serving: Cal 336; Prot 20 g; Carbo 2 g; Fiber <1 g; T Fat 27 g; Chol 177 mg; Sod 1652 mg.

Spicy Shrimp with Walnuts

Yield: 6 servings   Utensil: wok   Preheat: 250 degrees

1 cup walnut halves
½ cup soy sauce
¼ cup vegetable oil
½ cup dry sherry
2 tablespoons sesame oil
1½ tablespoons sugar
8 dried chili peppers, chopped
2 tablespoons minced garlic
2 tablespoons fresh minced ginger
3 pounds large fresh shrimp, peeled
2 tablespoons peanut oil
1½ bunches green onions, sliced into 1½-inch pieces

Place walnuts on baking sheet. Toast in oven at 250 degrees for 15 minutes. Combine soy sauce, vegetable oil, sherry, sesame oil, sugar, chili peppers, garlic and ginger in large bowl; mix well. Add shrimp, stirring to coat with marinade. Marinate in refrigerator for 30 minutes to 1½ hours. Drain, reserving marinade. Stir-fry shrimp in hot peanut oil in wok for 3 to 4 minutes or until shrimp turn pink. Remove to warm platter. Pour reserved marinade and toasted walnuts into wok. Bring to a boil. Cook until mixture becomes syrupy, stirring constantly. Add shrimp and green onions, tossing to coat. Serve with cooked rice.

Approx Per Serving: Cal 487; Prot 43 g; Carbo 16 g; Fiber 3 g; T Fat 26 g; Chol 354 mg; Sod 1787 mg.

Vegetables
and
Side Dishes

Beefy Baked Beans

Yield: 10 servings   Utensil: baking dish   Preheat: 350 degrees

1 32-ounce can pork and beans
1/3 cup catsup
3/4 cup packed brown sugar
6 slices crisp-fried bacon, crumbled
1 pound ground beef
1 small onion, minced

Combine pork and beans, catsup, brown sugar and bacon in 2-quart baking dish. Brown ground beef and onion in skillet, stirring until ground beef is crumbly; drain. Add to bean mixture; mix well. Bake at 350 degrees for 30 minutes.

Approx Per Serving: Cal 290; Prot 15 g; Carbo 38 g; Fiber 5 g; T Fat 10 g; Chol 39 mg; Sod 492 mg.

Au Gratin Carrots

Yield: 10 servings   Utensil: baking dish   Preheat: 350 degrees

1/3 cup chopped onion
3 tablespoons butter
3 tablespoons flour
1 1/2 teaspoons salt
1/8 teaspoon pepper
1 1/2 cups milk
1 cup cubed Velveeta cheese
4 cups sliced carrots, cooked, drained
1 tablespoon parsley
2 cups bread crumbs
1 tablespoon melted butter

Sauté onion in 3 tablespoons butter in skillet. Stir in flour, salt and pepper. Add milk gradually, stirring constantly. Cook until thickened, stirring constantly. Add cheese, stirring constantly until melted. Stir in carrots and parsley. Spoon into 1 1/2-quart baking dish. Sprinkle with mixture of bread crumbs and remaining 1 tablespoon butter. Bake at 350 degrees for 20 minutes.

Approx Per Serving: Cal 213; Prot 7 g; Carbo 23 g; Fiber 2 g; T Fat 11 g; Chol 29 mg; Sod 698 mg.

Carrot and Rice Ring

Yield: 6 servings Utensil: ring mold Preheat: 350 degrees

3 cups cooked rice
2 cups grated carrots
¼ cup grated onion
2 tablespoons flour
1 10-ounce can Cheddar cheese soup
1 egg, lightly beaten
1 teaspoon salt
¼ teaspoon pepper
1 teaspoon Worcestershire sauce
Dash of red hot sauce
1 10-ounce package frozen peas

Combine rice, carrots, onion and flour in large bowl. Add soup, egg, salt, pepper, Worcestershire sauce and hot sauce; mix well. Press mixture into well greased 8-inch ring mold. Bake at 350 degrees for 30 minutes. Cook peas using package directions; drain. Season to taste. Invert rice ring onto platter; fill center with peas.

Approx Per Serving: Cal 252; Prot 8 g; Carbo 42 g; Fiber 4 g; T Fat 6 g; Chol 47 mg; Sod 829 mg.

Elegant Scalloped Corn

Yield: 8 servings Utensil: baking dish Preheat: 350 degrees

1 16-ounce can corn
1 cup cracker crumbs
1 teaspoon salt
2 tablespoons melted butter
¼ cup chopped onion
¼ cup chopped green bell pepper
¼ cup chopped celery
¾ cup shredded American cheese
2 eggs, well beaten
1 cup milk
¼ cup cracker crumbs
1 tablespoon melted butter
¼ teaspoon paprika

Combine corn, 1 cup cracker crumbs, salt, 2 tablespoons butter, onion, green pepper, celery, cheese, eggs and milk in large bowl; mix well. Pour into greased 6x10-inch baking dish. Top with mixture of ¼ cup cracker crumbs and 1 tablespoon butter; sprinkle with paprika. Bake at 350 degrees for 35 minutes or until set.

Approx Per Serving: Cal 222; Prot 7 g; Carbo 23 g; Fiber 1 g; T Fat 12 g; Chol 83 mg; Sod 782 mg.

Corn Pudding

Yield: 12 servings   Utensil: baking dish   Preheat: 350 degrees

1 16-ounce can whole kernel corn
1 egg
1 cup sour cream
1 7-ounce package corn bread mix
1 16-ounce can cream-style corn
1/2 cup melted margarine

Drain whole kernel corn, reserving liquid. Beat egg lightly in bowl. Add sour cream and a small amount of reserved corn liquid; mix well. Stir in corn bread mix, whole kernel corn, remaining reserved corn liquid and undrained cream-style corn, mixing well after each addition. Stir in margarine. Pour into 2-quart baking dish. Bake at 350 degrees for 1 hour.

Approx Per Serving: Cal 201; Prot 3 g; Carbo 20 g; Fiber 2 g; T Fat 13 g; Chol 26 mg; Sod 371 mg.

Golden Baked Onions

Yield: 8 servings   Utensil: baking dish   Preheat: 350 degrees

1/2 cup butter
6 medium onions, thinly sliced
1 10-ounce can cream of chicken soup
1 cup milk
Salt and pepper to taste
12 ounces Gruyère cheese, shredded
8 slices French bread

Melt butter in large skillet over medium heat. Add onions. Cook for 15 minutes or until tender. Reserve butter and pan juices in skillet. Transfer onions to 2-quart baking dish coated with nonstick cooking spray. Pour mixture of soup, milk, salt and pepper over onions. Sprinkle with cheese. Dip 1 side of bread slices in reserved butter. Arrange bread slices buttered side up over cheese layer. Bake at 350 degrees for 30 minutes or until golden brown. May substitute Swiss cheese for Gruyère cheese.

Approx Per Serving: Cal 471; Prot 20 g; Carbo 31 g; Fiber 3 g; T Fat 30 g; Chol 85 mg; Sod 757 mg.

Pea Casserole

Yield: 6 servings   Utensil: baking dish   Preheat: 350 degrees

1 16-ounce package frozen peas, thawed
1/2 cup crumbled crisp-fried bacon
1 8-ounce can water chestnuts, drained, chopped
1/4 cup chopped onion
1/4 cup sherry
1 cup cream of celery soup
1/2 to 1 cup stuffing mix
2 tablespoons melted butter

Spread peas in 1-quart baking dish. Combine bacon, water chestnuts, onion, sherry and soup in bowl; mix well. Pour over peas; mix lightly. Sprinkle with stuffing mix; drizzle with butter. Bake at 350 degrees for 30 minutes. May add 1/4 cup sherry to soup mixture.

Approx Per Serving: Cal 306; Prot 12 g; Carbo 27 g; Fiber 5 g; T Fat 16 g; Chol 31 mg; Sod 895 mg.

Cheese Potatoes

Yield: 12 servings   Utensil: baking dish   Preheat: 350 degrees

1 32-ounce package frozen hashed brown potatoes, thawed
1/2 cup melted margarine
1/2 cup chopped onion
1 10-ounce can cream of chicken soup
1 cup sour cream
1 cup milk
2 cups shredded mild Cheddar cheese
1/2 teaspoon salt
1/4 teaspoon pepper
1/4 cup melted butter
2 cups crushed cornflakes

Place hashed brown potatoes in greased 9x13-inch baking dish. Combine margarine, onion, soup, sour cream, milk, cheese, salt and pepper in bowl; mix well. Pour over potatoes. Sprinkle with mixture of melted butter and cornflakes. Bake at 350 degrees for 1 hour.

Approx Per Serving: Cal 447; Prot 9 g; Carbo 32 g; Fiber 2 g; T Fat 33 g; Chol 43 mg; Sod 660 mg.

CREAMY POTATO BAKE

Yield: 8 servings   Utensil: baking pan   Preheat: 350 degrees

1 cup sour cream
1 cup milk
1 cup cottage cheese
6 ounces cream cheese with chives, softened
6 cups diced cooked potatoes
1½ teaspoons salt
¼ teaspoon pepper
1 teaspoon dillweed
1 cup chopped green onions with tops
1 cup shredded Cheddar cheese
8 slices crisp-fried bacon, crumbled

Combine sour cream, milk, cottage cheese and cream cheese in bowl; mix until consistency of sauce. Layer half the potatoes, half the salt, half the pepper, half the dillweed, half the green onions and half the Cheddar cheese in greased 9x13-inch baking pan. Pour half the sauce over layers. Repeat the layers. Sprinkle with bacon. Bake at 350 degrees for 35 to 40 minutes or until bubbly.

Approx Per Serving: Cal 443; Prot 16 g; Carbo 43 g; Fiber 4 g; T Fat 24 g; Chol 64 mg; Sod 798 mg.

ITALIAN POTATOES

Yield: 6 servings   Utensil: baking dish   Preheat: 350 degrees

4 large or 6 medium russet potatoes
½ cup fine bread crumbs, toasted
½ cup grated Parmesan cheese
2 or 3 large tomatoes, thinly sliced
2 large red onions, thinly sliced into rings
1½ teaspoons oregano
1 teaspoon salt
Pepper to taste
½ cup olive oil

Peel potatoes; cut into wedges lengthwise. Place in bowl of cold water. Combine bread crumbs and Parmesan cheese in plastic bag. Drain potatoes; do not dry. Coat potatoes with crumb mixture. Arrange potatoes in shallow 9x13-inch baking dish; sprinkle with any remaining crumb mixture. Place tomato slices and onion rings over potatoes. Sprinkle with oregano, salt and pepper. Drizzle with oil just before baking. Bake at 350 degrees for 1 hour and 10 minutes or just until potatoes are brown.

Approx Per Serving: Cal 401; Prot 8 g; Carbo 47 g; Fiber 5 g; T Fat 21 g; Chol 6 mg; Sod 563 mg.

Sauerkraut Casserole

Yield: 6 servings   Utensil: Dutch oven   Preheat: 350 degrees

1 medium onion, chopped
Bacon drippings for sautéing
1 16-ounce can sauerkraut, drained
1 16-ounce can tomatoes
½ cup sugar
4 or 5 slices crisp-fried bacon, crumbled

Sauté onion in bacon drippings in Dutch oven until transparent. Add sauerkraut, undrained tomatoes, sugar and bacon, stirring after each addition. Bake at 350 degrees for 45 minutes.

Approx Per Serving: Cal 132; Prot 3 g; Carbo 25 g; Fiber 3 g; T Fat 3 g; Chol 4 mg; Sod 708 mg.
Nutritional information does not include bacon drippings.

Spinach Soufflé

Yield: 8 servings   Utensil: casserole   Preheat: 350 degrees

2 10-ounce packages frozen chopped spinach
1 10-ounce can cream of mushroom soup
1 cup reduced-calorie mayonnaise
1 cup shredded Cheddar cheese
2 eggs, beaten
3 tablespoons minced onion
½ cup bread crumbs
1 tablespoon melted butter

Cook spinach using package directions; drain. Let stand until cool. Combine soup, mayonnaise, cheese, eggs and onion in bowl; mix well. Stir in spinach. Spoon into greased casserole. Sprinkle with mixture of bread crumbs and butter. Bake at 350 degrees for 30 to 40 minutes or until set.

Approx Per Serving: Cal 229; Prot 8 g; Carbo 12 g; Fiber 2 g; T Fat 16 g; Chol 81 mg; Sod 624 mg.

Candied Sweet Potatoes

Yield: 12 servings   Utensil: electric skillet   Preheat: 320 degrees

¼ cup butter
1 cup packed brown sugar
¼ cup orange juice
½ teaspoon salt
1 teaspoon grated orange rind
¼ teaspoon cinnamon
4 to 6 boiled sweet potatoes, cut into halves

Combine butter, brown sugar, orange juice, salt, orange rind and cinnamon in electric skillet. Cook at 320 degrees until mixture reaches the boiling point. Boil for 2 minutes, stirring constantly. Place sweet potatoes in hot mixture. Simmer at 220 degrees for 10 minutes. Spoon syrup over sweet potatoes and turn frequently.

Approx Per Serving: Cal 163; Prot 1 g; Carbo 32 g; Fiber 2 g; T Fat 4 g; Chol 10 mg; Sod 135 mg.

Tomato Pie

Yield: 8 servings   Utensil: baking dish   Preheat: 375 degrees

6 medium tomatoes
2 cups baking mix
½ cup milk
2 tablespoons basil
Salt and pepper to taste
¾ cup mayonnaise
½ cup shredded Cheddar cheese

Peel tomatoes; cut into large bite-sized pieces. Let stand in strainer to drain. Combine baking mix and milk in 8x11-inch baking dish; mix well. Press mixture over bottom and sides of pan. Fill with tomatoes. Sprinkle with basil, salt and pepper. Spread mixture of mayonnaise and cheese over top. Bake at 375 degrees for 30 minutes.

Approx Per Serving: Cal 340; Prot 6 g; Carbo 26 g; Fiber 1 g; T Fat 24 g; Chol 22 mg; Sod 572 mg.

Zucchini Casserole

Yield: 8 servings   Utensil: baking dish   Preheat: 350 degrees

1 medium onion, chopped
1 medium green bell pepper, chopped
1 pound fresh mushrooms, sliced
2 medium zucchini, peeled, sliced
Garlic powder to taste
Salt and pepper to taste
1 28-ounce can whole peeled tomatoes
2 cups seasoned croutons
8 to 10 ounces sliced Swiss cheese

Sauté onion, green pepper, mushrooms and zucchini in skillet sprayed with nonstick cooking spray until tender. Season with garlic powder, salt and pepper. Add undrained tomatoes. Simmer, covered, for 10 to 15 minutes, stirring occasionally. Layer half the croutons, half the vegetable mixture and half the Swiss cheese in 2-quart baking dish. Repeat layers. Bake at 350 degrees for 1 hour or until golden brown. May be baked at 250 degrees for 1 1/2 to 2 hours to enhance flavor. Cover with foil if cheese begins to brown too much.

Approx Per Serving: Cal 212; Prot 13 g; Carbo 15 g; Fiber 3 g; T Fat 12 g; Chol 32 mg; Sod 335 mg.

Zucchini-Pepper Sauté

Yield: 4 servings   Utensil: serving dish   Preheat: no

2 large green bell peppers, chopped
1 large zucchini, peeled, chopped
1 medium onion, chopped
3 or 4 stalks celery, chopped
1 6-ounce can tomato paste
1/2 teaspoon oregano
1/4 teaspoon garlic salt
2 to 3 tablespoons sugar
1/8 teaspoon lemon pepper
1/4 cup grated Romano cheese

Sauté green peppers, zucchini, onion and celery each separately in skillet sprayed with nonstick cooking spray until tender. Place in 8-inch round serving dish. Combine tomato paste, oregano, garlic salt, sugar and lemon pepper in skillet. Cook until heated through. Pour over vegetables; mix well. Sprinkle cheese over top. Serve immediately. May substitute red bell pepper for green.

Approx Per Serving: Cal 141; Prot 6 g; Carbo 28 g; Fiber 5 g; T Fat 2 g; Chol 6 mg; Sod 267 mg.

Swiss Vegetable Combo

Yield: 8 servings	Utensil: baking dish	Preheat: 350 degrees

1 16-ounce package frozen broccoli, carrots and cauliflower
1 stalk celery, chopped
1 10-ounce can cream of mushroom soup
1 cup shredded Swiss cheese
⅓ cup sour cream
¼ teaspoon pepper
1 4-ounce jar chopped pimentos, drained
1 3-ounce can French-fried onions

Thaw broccoli, carrots and cauliflower; drain. Combine with celery, soup, half the cheese, sour cream, pepper, pimentos and half the fried onions in large bowl; mix well. Pour into 1-quart baking dish. Bake, covered, at 350 degrees for 30 minutes. Top with remaining cheese and remaining fried onions. Bake, uncovered, for 5 minutes longer.

Approx Per Serving: Cal 183; Prot 7 g; Carbo 16 g; Fiber 3 g; T Fat 11 g; Chol 21 mg; Sod 391 mg.

Cranberry Relish

Yield: 30 servings	Utensil: saucepan	Preheat: no

1 5¼-ounce can pineapple tidbits
½ cup (about) orange juice
1 12-ounce package cranberries
1 cup sugar
¾ cup golden raisins
½ teaspoon cinnamon
¼ teaspoon allspice
½ teaspoon ground ginger
Salt to taste
¾ cup chopped walnuts

Drain pineapple, reserving liquid. Add enough orange juice to reserved pineapple liquid to measure 1¼ cups. Pour mixture into saucepan with cranberries, sugar, raisins, cinnamon, allspice, ginger and salt. Cook just until ¼ of the cranberries pop open. Remove from heat; cool. Add pineapple and walnuts; mix well. Pour into serving bowl. Chill until serving time.

Approx Per Serving: Cal 68; Prot 1 g; Carbo 13 g; Fiber 1 g; T Fat 2 g; Chol 0 mg; Sod 1 mg.

Scalloped Pineapple

Yield: 8 servings   Utensil: baking dish   Preheat: 350 degrees

3 eggs, well beaten
1/4 cup melted butter
Salt to taste
1 cup sugar
1 16-ounce can crushed pineapple or tidbits
4 cups fresh bread cubes

Combine eggs, butter and salt in bowl; mix well. Stir in sugar, undrained pineapple and bread cubes. Spoon into buttered 2-quart baking dish. Bake at 350 degrees for 35 to 40 minutes or until set.

Approx Per Serving: Cal 281; Prot 4 g; Carbo 48 g; Fiber 1 g; T Fat 9 g; Chol 95 mg; Sod 191 mg.

Chinese Fried Rice

Yield: 6 servings   Utensil: skillet   Preheat: no

4 to 6 slices bacon
3 cups cooked rice
2 or 3 eggs, beaten
2 tablespoons soy sauce
Pepper to taste
1 6-ounce can shrimp

Fry bacon in large skillet until crisp. Drain on paper towels; crumble. Stir-fry rice in bacon drippings in skillet for 5 minutes. Add eggs and bacon. Stir-fry until eggs are set. Season with soy sauce and pepper. Add shrimp. Stir-fry until heated through.

Approx Per Serving: Cal 224; Prot 14 g; Carbo 26 g; Fiber <1 g; T Fat 7 g; Chol 161 mg; Sod 526 mg.

Wild Rice Pilaf

Yield: 4 servings   Utensil: saucepan   Preheat: no

1/4 cup strong chicken broth
1 small onion, finely chopped
1 clove of garlic, minced
1 teaspoon lemon rind, minced
1 cup uncooked wild rice
1 3/4 cups strong chicken broth
2 tablespoons toasted sesame seed

Bring 1/4 cup broth to a boil in saucepan. Add onion and garlic. Cook just until tender. Add lemon rind and rice; mix well. Add remaining 1 3/4 cups broth. Bring to a boil. Reduce heat to low. Simmer, covered, for 1 hour and 5 minutes to 1 hour and 15 minutes or until rice is very tender. Stir in sesame seed. Garnish with parsley if desired.

Approx Per Serving: Cal 226; Prot 7 g; Carbo 41 g; Fiber 1 g; T Fat 4 g; Chol 1 mg; Sod 393 mg.

SIMPLE RICE

Yield: 8 servings   Utensil: baking dish   Preheat: 350 degrees

1 cup uncooked rice
1 14-ounce can beef consommé
1 4-ounce can mushrooms
1 10-ounce can French onion soup
½ cup melted margarine

Combine rice, consommé, mushrooms, soup and margarine in bowl; mix well. Pour into 1½-quart baking dish. Bake, covered, at 350 degrees for 45 minutes to 1 hour or until rice is tender.

Approx Per Serving: Cal 209; Prot 4 g; Carbo 22 g; Fiber 1 g; T Fat 12 g; Chol <1 mg; Sod 647 mg.

MUSTARD SAUCE

Yield: 15 servings   Utensil: saucepan   Preheat: no

1 egg yolk, lightly beaten
⅓ cup sugar
⅓ cup prepared mustard
⅓ cup butter
⅓ cup mayonnaise
1 teaspoon dry mustard
2 tablespoons vinegar

Combine egg, sugar, prepared mustard, butter, mayonnaise, dry mustard and vinegar in saucepan. Bring mixture to a boil. Cook for 1 minute, stirring constantly. Cool slightly. Store, covered, in refrigerator.

Approx Per Serving: Cal 96; Prot 1 g; Carbo 5 g; Fiber <1 g; T Fat 9 g; Chol 28 mg; Sod 131 mg.

RAREBIT TOPPING

Yield: 50 servings   Utensil: double boiler   Preheat: no

2 tablespoons butter
2 tablespoons flour
1 teaspoon salt
¼ teaspoon dry mustard
1 tablespoon Worcestershire sauce
2 cups milk
1 pound American cheese, cut into pieces

Melt butter in double boiler. Blend in flour, salt, mustard and Worcestershire sauce. Bring to a boil. Stir in milk gradually, stirring constantly. Cook until thickened, stirring constantly. Cook for 1 minute longer. Stir in cheese. Cook just until cheese is melted, stirring constantly. Serve on hamburgers.

Approx Per Serving: Cal 45; Prot 2 g; Carbo 1 g; Fiber <1 g; T Fat 4 g; Chol 11 mg; Sod 183 mg.

Breads

Cinnamon Delight

Yield: 8 servings　　　　Utensil: tube pan　　　　Preheat: 350 degrees

½ cup shortening
¾ cup sugar
1 teaspoon vanilla extract
3 eggs
2 cups sifted flour
1 teaspoon baking powder
1 teaspoon soda
1 cup sour cream
6 tablespoons butter, softened
1 cup packed brown sugar
2 teaspoons cinnamon
1 cup chopped pecans

Cream shortening, sugar and vanilla in bowl until light and fluffy. Add eggs 1 at a time, beating well after each addition. Sift flour, baking powder and soda together. Add to creamed mixture alternately with sour cream, beating well after each addition. Pour half the batter into greased and waxed paper-lined 10-inch tube pan. Blend butter, brown sugar and cinnamon in small bowl. Stir in pecans until crumbly. Sprinkle half the mixture over batter. Top with remaining batter; sprinkle with remaining pecan mixture. Bake at 350 degrees for 30 to 40 minutes or until top springs back when lightly touched. May serve warm or cool.

Approx Per Serving: Cal 660; Prot 7 g; Carbo 71 g; Fiber 2 g; T Fat 40 g; Chol 116 mg; Sod 271 mg.

Dutch Apple Bread

Yield: 12 servings　　　　Utensil: loaf pan　　　　Preheat: 350 degrees

½ cup butter, softened
1 cup sugar
2 eggs
1 teaspoon vanilla extract
2 cups flour
1 teaspoon soda
½ teaspoon salt
1 cup chopped apple
⅓ cup sour milk
½ cup chopped walnuts
½ cup cranberries

Cream butter and sugar in bowl until light and fluffy. Add eggs and vanilla; mix well. Combine flour, soda and salt in small bowl. Add to creamed mixture alternately with mixture of apple and milk, stirring after each addition. Fold in walnuts and cranberries gently. Spoon into greased and floured loaf pan. Bake at 350 degrees for 55 minutes. Serve with whipped cream cheese. May substitute orange juice for sour milk.

Approx Per Serving: Cal 266; Prot 4 g; Carbo 36 g; Fiber 1 g; T Fat 12 g; Chol 57 mg; Sod 237 mg.

Prize Banana Nut Bread

Yield: 12 servings   Utensil: loaf pan   Preheat: 300 degrees

2 large bananas, mashed
1 cup sugar
2 eggs
3 tablespoons milk
2 cups flour
1/4 teaspoon salt
1/2 teaspoon soda
1/2 teaspoon baking powder
1/2 cup melted butter
1 teaspoon vanilla extract
1/2 cup chopped pecans

Blend bananas, sugar and eggs in bowl. Add milk; mix well. Mix flour, salt, soda and baking powder together. Add to creamed mixture; mix well. Stir in butter, vanilla and pecans. Pour into greased and floured loaf pan. Bake at 300 degrees for 60 minutes.

Approx Per Serving: Cal 274; Prot 4 g; Carbo 38 g; Fiber 1 g; T Fat 12 g; Chol 57 mg; Sod 171 mg.

Beer Bread

Yield: 12 servings   Utensil: loaf pan   Preheat: 350 degrees

3 cups self-rising flour
2 tablespoons sugar
1 8-ounce bottle of beer, at room temperature
1 tablespoon melted butter

Combine flour and sugar in large bowl. Pour in beer; mix well. Dough will be sticky. Transfer dough to greased loaf pan. Bake at 350 degrees for 1 hour and 10 minutes. Brush top of bread with butter half way through baking time.

Approx Per Serving: Cal 134; Prot 3 g; Carbo 26 g; Fiber 1 g; T Fat 1 g; Chol 3 mg; Sod 346 mg.

Dilly Bread

Yield: 6 servings	Utensil: loaf pan	Preheat: 350 degrees

1 envelope dry yeast
1/4 cup warm water
1 cup cream-style cottage cheese
1 tablespoon butter, softened
1/4 teaspoon soda
1 teaspoon salt
1 tablespoon onion flakes
2 teaspoons dillseed
1 egg
2 1/4 to 2 1/2 cups sifted flour

Dissolve yeast in warm water in large bowl. Add cottage cheese, butter, soda, salt, onion flakes, dillseed and egg; mix well. Add flour gradually, mixing well after each addition. Knead on floured surface until smooth and elastic. Place in greased loaf pan. Let rise, covered, in warm place until doubled in bulk. Bake at 350 degrees for 30 to 45 minutes or until golden brown.

Approx Per Serving: Cal 244; Prot 11 g; Carbo 38 g; Fiber 2 g; T Fat 5 g; Chol 46 mg; Sod 560 mg.

Orange Pecan Bread

Yield: 12 servings	Utensil: loaf pan	Preheat: 350 degrees

1/2 cup butter, softened
3/4 cup sugar
2 egg yolks
Grated rind of 1 orange
1 1/2 cups flour
1 1/2 teaspoons baking powder
1/4 teaspoon soda
1/2 cup orange juice
1 cup chopped pecans
2 egg whites, stiffly beaten
1/4 cup orange juice
1/4 cup sugar

Cream butter and 3/4 cup sugar in mixer bowl until light and fluffy. Add egg yolks 1 at a time, mixing well after each addition. Add orange rind; mix well. Sift flour, baking powder and soda together. Add to creamed mixture alternately with 1/2 cup orange juice, beginning and ending with flour mixture. Mix well after each addition. Stir in pecans. Fold in egg whites gently. Pour into greased loaf pan. Bake at 350 degrees for 50 to 60 minutes or until bread tests done. Combine remaining 1/4 cup orange juice and remaining 1/4 cup sugar in small saucepan. Simmer for 5 minutes or until light syrup is formed, stirring occasionally. Spoon over hot bread. Cool in pan on wire rack.

Approx Per Serving: Cal 276; Prot 4 g; Carbo 32 g; Fiber 1 g; T Fat 16 g; Chol 56 mg; Sod 135 mg.

Pineapple Bread

Yield: 12 servings Utensil: loaf pan Preheat: 350 degrees

2½ cups flour
½ cup sugar
4 teaspoons baking powder
1 teaspoon salt
½ cup wheat germ
1 egg, beaten
⅓ cup butter, softened
⅓ cup milk
1 8-ounce can crushed pineapple

Combine flour, sugar, baking powder and salt in large bowl. Stir in wheat germ. Add egg, butter, milk and undrained pineapple; mix well. Batter will be stiff. Pour into greased loaf pan. Let stand for 15 minutes before baking. Bake at 350 degrees for 55 to 60 minutes or until bread tests done. Cool in pan for 10 minutes. Remove to wire rack to cool completely.

Approx Per Serving: Cal 207; Prot 4 g; Carbo 33 g; Fiber 1 g; T Fat 6 g; Chol 32 mg; Sod 339 mg.

Pumpkin Date Bread

Yield: 24 servings Utensil: 2 loaf pans Preheat: 350 degrees

3 cups sugar
1 cup oil
4 eggs, beaten
2 cups pumpkin
3½ cups flour
2 teaspoons soda
¾ teaspoon baking powder
1½ teaspoons salt
1 teaspoon cinnamon
1 teaspoon nutmeg
1 teaspoon cloves
1 teaspoon allspice
1 teaspoon ginger
⅓ cup water
⅓ cup bourbon
1 teaspoon vanilla extract
1 cup chopped dates

Mix sugar and oil in large bowl. Add eggs and pumpkin; mix well. Sift flour, soda, baking powder, salt, cinnamon, nutmeg, cloves, allspice and ginger together. Add to pumpkin mixture alternately with water and bourbon, mixing well after each addition. Stir in vanilla and dates. Pour into 2 well greased and floured 5x9-inch loaf pans. Bake at 350 degrees for 1 hour and 30 minutes or until bread tests done. Cool in pans for 10 minutes. Remove to wire rack to cool completely. May omit dates or substitute raisins or nuts.

Approx Per Serving: Cal 291; Prot 3 g; Carbo 46 g; Fiber 1 g; T Fat 10 g; Chol 36 mg; Sod 226 mg.

Strawberry Bread

Yield: 24 servings	Utensil: 2 loaf pans	Preheat: 350 degrees

3 cups flour
2 cups sugar
1 teaspoon salt
1 teaspoon cinnamon
4 eggs, beaten
1¼ cups vegetable oil
2 10-ounce packages frozen strawberries, thawed

Mix flour, sugar, salt and cinnamon in large bowl. Make well in center of mixture. Combine eggs, oil and strawberries in bowl; mix well. Add to well in dry ingredients; mix well. Spoon into 2 greased and floured loaf pans. Bake at 350 degrees for 1 hour. Cool in pans for 10 minutes. Remove to wire rack to cool completely.

Approx Per Serving: Cal 243; Prot 3 g; Carbo 31 g; Fiber 1 g; T Fat 13 g; Chol 36 mg; Sod 102 mg.

Honey Whole Wheat Bread

Yield: 36 servings	Utensil: 3 loaf pans	Preheat: 350 degrees

3 cups warm water
½ cup honey
2 envelopes dry yeast
4 cups whole wheat flour
½ cup nonfat dry milk
1 tablespoon salt
2 tablespoons oil
4 to 4½ cups all-purpose flour

Combine water, honey and yeast in large bowl; stir until yeast is dissolved. Add 3 cups whole wheat flour, milk powder, salt and oil to yeast mixture, stirring until smooth. Add remaining 1 cup whole wheat flour and enough all-purpose flour to make soft and workable dough. Knead on floured surface until smooth and elastic. Place in greased bowl, turning to grease surface. Let rise, covered, in warm place until doubled in bulk. Punch dough down. Knead for 1 minute. Divide dough into 3 portions; shape into loaves. Place in 3 greased loaf pans. Let rise, covered, until dough is just over top of pan. Bake at 350 degrees for 35 to 40 minutes or until bread tests done. Remove from pans. Cool on wire rack.

Approx Per Serving: Cal 120; Prot 4 g; Carbo 25 g; Fiber 2 g; T Fat 1 g; Chol <1 mg; Sod 184 mg.

Banana Oatbran Muffins

Yield: 12 servings   Utensil: muffin pan   Preheat: 425 degrees

1½ cups Bran Buds cereal
1½ cups oat bran cereal
1 tablespoon baking powder
¼ cup packed brown sugar
1½ cups skim milk
2 tablespoons vegetable oil
2 very ripe bananas
2 egg whites

Mix Bran Buds cereal, oat bran cereal, baking powder and brown sugar in large bowl. Combine milk, oil, bananas and egg whites in blender container. Process until smooth. Add to dry mixture; mix well. Fill paper-lined muffin cups with batter. Bake at 425 degrees for 18 minutes. Remove to wire rack to cool.

Approx Per Serving: Cal 125; Prot 4 g; Carbo 24 g; Fiber 4 g; T Fat 4 g; Chol 1 mg; Sod 223 mg.

Bran Muffins

Yield: 60 servings   Utensil: muffin pans   Preheat: 350 degrees

4 eggs, beaten
1 cup oil
3 cups sugar
4 cups buttermilk
1 15-ounce package raisin bran cereal
5 cups flour
2 teaspoons salt
5 teaspoons soda

Combine eggs, oil, sugar, buttermilk and cereal in large bowl; mix well. Mix flour, salt and soda in bowl. Add to buttermilk mixture, stirring until just mixed. Fill greased muffin cups ⅔ full. Bake at 350 degrees for 20 to 25 minutes or until muffins test done. Remove from pan. Cool on wire rack. May store batter in refrigerator for up to 3 months. May add pecans before baking.

Approx Per Serving: Cal 144; Prot 3 g; Carbo 25 g; Fiber 1 g; T Fat 4 g; Chol 15 mg; Sod 204 mg.

SASSY CINNAMON MUFFINS

Yield: 10 servings	Utensil: muffin pan	Preheat: 400 degrees

1½ cups flour
¼ cup sugar
¼ cup packed brown sugar
2 teaspoons baking powder
1 teaspoon salt
½ teaspoon cinnamon
1 egg, beaten
½ cup milk
½ cup oil

Sift flour, sugar, brown sugar, baking powder, salt and cinnamon together. Combine egg and milk in large bowl. Add oil; mix well. Add dry mixture, stirring just until moistened. Fill muffin cups ⅔ full. Bake at 400 degrees for 20 to 25 minutes or until muffins test done.

Approx Per Serving: Cal 221; Prot 3 g; Carbo 25 g; Fiber 1 g; T Fat 12 g; Chol 23 mg; Sod 294 mg.

PUMPKIN APPLE STREUSEL MUFFINS

Yield: 18 servings	Utensil: muffin pan	Preheat: 350 degrees

2½ cups flour
1¾ cups sugar
1 tablespoon pumpkin pie spice
1 teaspoon soda
½ teaspoon salt
3 egg whites, lightly beaten
1 cup pumpkin
½ cup vegetable oil
2 cups finely chopped peeled apples
2 tablespoons flour
¼ cup sugar
½ teaspoon cinnamon
4 teaspoons margarine

Mix flour, sugar, pumpkin pie spice, soda and salt in large bowl. Combine egg whites, pumpkin and oil in medium bowl; mix well. Add to dry mixture, stirring just until moistened. Stir in apples. Fill greased muffin cups ¾ full. Combine remaining 2 tablespoons flour, remaining ¼ cup sugar and cinnamon in small bowl. Cut in margarine until crumbly. Sprinkle over batter in muffin cups. Bake at 350 degrees for 35 to 40 minutes or until muffins test done.

Approx Per Serving: Cal 228; Prot 3 g; Carbo 39 g; Fiber 1 g; T Fat 7 g; Chol 0 mg; Sod 125 mg.

Yogurt Date Muffins

Yield: 12 servings   Utensil: muffin pan   Preheat: 400 degrees

1/2 cup chopped dates
1/4 cup water
2 eggs
1 cup plain yogurt
1/4 cup oil
1/2 cup sugar
3/4 cup all-purpose flour
3/4 cup whole wheat flour
1 1/2 teaspoons soda
1/2 teaspoon salt
1/2 cup toasted wheat germ
1/2 cup flaked coconut
1/2 cup pecans

Soak dates in water until softened. Beat eggs in large bowl. Add yogurt and oil; mix well. Combine sugar, all-purpose flour, whole wheat flour, soda, salt, wheat germ, coconut and pecans in bowl. Add to yogurt mixture, stirring just until moistened. Stir in date mixture. Fill greased muffin cups 2/3 full. Bake at 400 degrees for 18 to 20 minutes or until muffins test done. May substitute fruit-flavored yogurt for plain yogurt.

Approx Per Serving: Cal 230; Prot 5 g; Carbo 30 g; Fiber 3 g; T Fat 11 g; Chol 37 mg; Sod 156 mg.

Mom's Pizza Crust

Yield: 16 servings   Utensil: 2 pizza pans   Preheat: 425 degrees

1 cup flour
1 envelope dry yeast
1 cup warm water
1 1/2 cups flour
1 1/2 teaspoons sugar
1 1/2 teaspoons salt
2 tablespoons oil

Combine 1 cup flour, yeast and water in bowl; mix well. Add remaining 1 1/2 cups flour, sugar, salt and oil; mix well. Let rise until doubled in bulk. Divide into 2 portions; pat into greased pizza pans. Bake at 425 degrees for 15 to 20 minutes or until light brown. May top with desired sauce, toppings and cheese. Bake until cheese is melted. May freeze partially baked crusts for later use.

Approx Per Serving: Cal 89; Prot 2 g; Carbo 15 g; Fiber 1 g; T Fat 2 g; Chol 0 mg; Sod 201 mg.

Hot Cross Buns

Yield: 24 servings   Utensil: baking sheet   Preheat: 350 degrees

1 envelope dry yeast
1 teaspoon sugar
2 tablespoons warm water
1/4 cup margarine
1 cup hot milk
5 tablespoons sugar
1 egg, lightly beaten
1/2 teaspoon salt
3 3/4 cups flour
1/4 cup melted margarine

Dissolve yeast and 1 teaspoon sugar in warm water. Add 1/4 cup margarine to milk in bowl. Let stand until lukewarm. Combine with yeast, remaining 5 tablespoons sugar, egg, salt and 2 cups flour in mixer bowl. Beat for 3 minutes. Add remaining flour; mix well. Let rise, covered, in warm place until doubled in bulk. Roll dough 1/2 inch thick on lightly floured surface. Cut into 3-inch circles. Let rise for 20 minutes. Arrange circles on 11x13-inch baking sheet. Brush half the circles with remaining 1/4 cup margarine; top with remaining circles. Let rise until doubled in bulk. Bake at 350 degrees for 30 minutes or until golden brown.

Approx Per Serving: Cal 126; Prot 3 g; Carbo 18 g; Fiber 1 g; T Fat 6 g; Chol 10 mg; Sod 93 mg.

Pull-Apart Rolls

Yield: 24 servings   Utensil: 2 loaf pans   Preheat: 350 degrees

2 loaves frozen bread dough
1 3-ounce package butterscotch instant pudding mix
1/2 cup packed brown sugar
1/2 cup butter, softened
1 teaspoon cinnamon
3/4 cup chopped pecans

Thaw dough partially; cut into 1-inch cubes. Combine pudding mix, brown sugar, butter, cinnamon and pecans in small bowl; mix until crumbly. Sprinkle a small amount of crumb mixture over bottoms of 2 buttered loaf pans. Alternate layers of bread cubes and crumb mixture in prepared pans until all ingredients are used. Let rise until doubled in bulk. Bake at 350 degrees for 30 minutes. Invert onto serving plates.

Approx Per Serving: Cal 139; Prot 2 g; Carbo 18 g; Fiber 1 g; T Fat 7 g; Chol 10 mg; Sod 154 mg.

Sweet Dough

Yield: 36 servings   Utensil: baking pan   Preheat: 425 degrees

2 envelopes dry yeast
1 cup lukewarm water
3/4 cup oil
1/2 cup sugar
2 teaspoons salt
2 cups milk, scalded
2 eggs, beaten
10 cups (about) flour
1 cup packed brown sugar
2 tablespoons light corn syrup
2/3 cup butter
1 cup chopped pecans

Dissolve yeast in water. Combine oil, sugar, salt and milk in large bowl. Let stand until cooled. Add yeast and eggs; beat well. Add enough flour to make soft dough. Let rise, covered, until doubled in bulk. Combine brown sugar, corn syrup, butter and pecans in saucepan. Cook over low heat, stirring until blended. Do not boil; mixture will be grainy. Pour into well greased 9x13-inch baking pan. Shape dough into rolls. Place on top of syrup mixture. Bake at 425 degrees for 10 minutes. Reduce oven temperature to 400 degrees. Bake for 10 minutes longer.

Approx Per Serving: Cal 269; Prot 5 g; Carbo 37 g; Fiber 1 g; T Fat 11 g; Chol 23 mg; Sod 161 mg.

Delicious Cheese Bread

Yield: 8 servings   Utensil: baking sheet   Preheat: 350 degrees

10 ounces Monterey Jack cheese, shredded
5 ounces mozzarella cheese, shredded
5 ounces mild Cheddar cheese, shredded
1 1/2 teaspoons garlic powder
1 1/2 cups mayonnaise
1 loaf French bread
Paprika to taste

Combine Monterey Jack cheese, mozzarella cheese, Cheddar cheese, garlic powder and mayonnaise in bowl; mix well. Slice bread lengthwise; spread with cheese mixture. Sprinkle with paprika. Place on baking sheet. Bake at 350 degrees for 20 minutes. Broil for 1 minute. Cut into thick slices. May make cheese mixture in advance.

Approx Per Serving: Cal 713; Prot 22 g; Carbo 31 g; Fiber 1 g; T Fat 55 g; Chol 89 mg; Sod 929 mg.

Mustard Bread

Yield: 10 servings   Utensil: baking sheet   Preheat: 425 degrees

1/4 cup prepared mustard
1/2 cup melted margarine
1/2 teaspoon minced onion
1 1/2 teaspoons poppy seed
Dash of Worcestershire sauce
2 12-ounce loaves French bread
8 ounces Swiss cheese, thinly sliced

Combine mustard, margarine, onion, poppy seed and Worcestershire sauce in small bowl; mix well. Slice bread to but not through bottom. Spread with mixture; place cheese slice between bread slices. Spread any remaining mixture on top of bread. Bake at 425 degrees for 15 minutes.

Approx Per Serving: Cal 366; Prot 13 g; Carbo 36 g; Fiber 1 g; T Fat 18 g; Chol 21 mg; Sod 639 mg.

Expand Your Bread-Baking Repertory

Change your favorite recipes with a change of flour for all or just a portion of the original flour measure.

- **All-purpose flour** is the mainstay of most baked goods. It is a blend of hard and soft wheats that have been milled, processed and bleached.
- **Unbleached flour** is all-purpose flour without the bleaching step. Use it interchangeably with all-purpose flour for a slightly heavier texture and heartier flavor.
- **Buckwheat flour** is a dark flour made from the seeds of the buckwheat plant. Substitute 1 cup buckwheat flour for about 1 1/3 to 1 1/2 cups all-purpose flour in recipes. Pancakes and waffles are especially good with this flour added.
- **Oat flour** can be purchased or you can make your own by processing old-fashioned oats in the blender or food processor until of coarse flour consistency. Substitute 1 cup oat flour for about 1 1/4 cups all-purpose flour.
- **Rye flour** is the dark distinctive-tasting flour made from rye grains. Most breads use rye flour for 1/3 to 1/2 the total amount of flour.
- **Self-rising flour** is a white flour containing leavening and salt. Do not use this for yeast breads. When using it in recipes calling for all-purpose flour, omit salt and baking powder.
- **Whole wheat or graham flour** is milled but unrefined wheat flour. It is rich in vitamins and fiber because it retains most of the bran. Substitute about 1 cup whole wheat flour for 1 1/3 cups all-purpose flour.

Desserts
Candy
and
Cookies

ALMOND CREAM SAUCE FOR ANGEL FOOD CAKE

Yield: 24 servings   Utensil: double boiler   Preheat: no

2 cups milk
1 cup sugar
2 eggs, well beaten
2 tablespoons cornstarch
2 tablespoons milk
2 tablespoons butter, softened
1 cup whipping cream, whipped
1 cup blanched, sliced, toasted almonds

Bring 2 cups milk and sugar to a boil in top of double boiler. Whisk in eggs. Dissolve cornstarch in 2 tablespoons milk. Stir into sauce. Add butter; mix well. Cook until sauce is thickened, stirring constantly. Cool. Fold in whipped cream and almonds just before serving.

Approx Per Serving: Cal 119; Prot 2 g; Carbo 11 g; Fiber <1 g; T Fat 8 g; Chol 37 mg; Sod 27 mg.

APPLE DUMPLINGS

Yield: 8 servings   Utensil: baking pan   Preheat: 425 degrees

2 cups flour
1 tablespoon baking powder
1/2 teaspoon salt
1 tablespoon sugar
6 tablespoons shortening
2/3 cup milk
8 small apples, peeled, cored
1/2 cup plus 1 tablespoon sugar
1 teaspoon cinnamon
1/2 teaspoon nutmeg
4 teaspoons butter
1 cup sugar
2 cups water
3 tablespoons butter
1/4 teaspoon cinnamon

Sift flour, baking powder, salt and 1 tablespoon sugar into large bowl. Cut in shortening until mixture is crumbly. Stir in milk gradually, working to form soft dough. Turn onto floured surface. Knead for 20 to 30 seconds. Roll out to 1/4-inch thickness. Cut into 8 squares. Place 1 apple in center of each square. Fill each cavity with 1 tablespoon sugar and 1/2 teaspoon butter. Sprinkle with mixture of 1 tablespoon sugar, 1 teaspoon cinnamon and nutmeg. Fold dough over to enclose apple, pinching edges to seal. Arrange in greased baking pan. Bake at 425 degrees for 20 minutes. Reduce temperature to 375 degrees. Bake for 20 minutes longer; cool. Combine remaining 1 cup sugar, water, 3 tablespoons butter and 1/4 teaspoon cinnamon in saucepan. Bring to a boil. Cook for 3 minutes, stirring constantly. Pour over apple dumplings.

Approx Per Serving: Cal 504; Prot 4 g; Carbo 87 g; Fiber 4 g; T Fat 17 g; Chol 20 mg; Sod 320 mg.

Apple Bavarian Torte

Yield: 8 servings　　　Utensil: springform pan　　　Preheat: 350 degrees

1 cup flour
1/3 cup sugar
1/2 teaspoon vanilla extract
1/2 cup butter, cut into pieces
1/2 cup sugar
16 ounces cream cheese, softened
1 teaspoon vanilla extract
2 eggs
2 large tart green apples, peeled, cored, thinly sliced
1/4 cup sugar
1/2 teaspoon cinnamon
1/2 teaspoon vanilla extract
1/3 cup coarsely chopped walnuts

Combine flour, 1/3 cup sugar and 1/2 teaspoon vanilla in medium bowl. Cut in butter until mixture is crumbly. Press in bottom and up side of 10-inch springform pan. Bake at 350 degrees for 5 minutes or until golden brown. Increase oven temperature to 450 degrees. Cream 1/2 cup sugar, cream cheese and 1 teaspoon vanilla in mixer bowl until light and fluffy. Add eggs 1 at a time, beating well after each addition. Spoon into prepared crust. Mix apples with 1/4 cup sugar, cinnamon and 1/2 teaspoon vanilla. Arrange over cream cheese layer. Sprinkle with walnuts. Bake at 450 degrees for 15 minutes. Reduce temperature to 350 degrees. Bake for 45 minutes longer or until knife inserted near center comes out clean. Cool in pan on rack. Chill in refrigerator. Let stand at room temperature for 30 minutes before serving.

Approx Per Serving: Cal 535; Prot 8 g; Carbo 47 g; Fiber 2 g; T Fat 36 g; Chol 146 mg; Sod 283 mg.

Buster Bar Dessert

Yield: 20 servings　　　Utensil: shallow dish　　　Preheat: no

2 cups confectioners' sugar
1 1/2 cups evaporated milk
2/3 cup semisweet chocolate chips
1/2 cup margarine
1 teaspoon vanilla extract
1 pound Oreo cookies, crushed
1/2 cup margarine, melted
1 cup Spanish peanuts
1/2 gallon vanilla ice cream, softened

Combine confectioners' sugar, evaporated milk, chocolate chips, 1/2 cup margarine and vanilla in saucepan. Cook over medium heat to 280 degrees on candy thermometer, soft-ball stage. Let cool completely. Combine cookies with 1/2 cup melted margarine in bowl. Press onto bottom of 9x13-inch dish. Cool in refrigerator. Layer peanuts, ice cream and chocolate mixture over prepared crumb crust. Freeze until ice cream is firm.

Approx Per Serving: Cal 442; Prot 7 g; Carbo 48 g; Fiber 1 g; T Fat 26 g; Chol 29 mg; Sod 313 mg.

Caramel Bar

Yield: 12 servings   Utensil: baking pan   Preheat: 325 degrees

1 cup flour
1/2 cup butter, softened
1/2 cup chopped pecans
1 cup confectioners' sugar
8 ounces cream cheese, softened
2 4-ounce packages caramel instant pudding mix
3 cups milk
8 ounces whipped topping

Mix flour, butter and pecans together in bowl. Press mixture onto bottom of 9x13-inch baking pan. Bake at 325 degrees for 10 minutes; cool. Cream confectioners' sugar and cream cheese in mixer bowl until light and fluffy. Spread over prepared crust. Prepare pudding using package directions, using only 3 cups milk. Spread over cream cheese mixture. Top with whipped topping.

Approx Per Serving: Cal 353; Prot 5 g; Carbo 37 g; Fiber 1 g; T Fat 21 g; Chol 50 mg; Sod 243 mg.

Bailey's Irish Cream Cheesecake

Yield: 12 servings   Utensil: springform pan   Preheat: 325 degrees

2 cups graham cracker crumbs
1/2 cup sugar
6 tablespoons melted butter
1 2/3 cups sugar
2 1/2 pounds cream cheese, softened
5 eggs
3/4 cup Bailey's Irish Cream
1 tablespoon vanilla extract
2 cups semisweet chocolate chips
1 cup whipping cream
2 tablespoons sugar
1 teaspoon instant coffee

Combine graham cracker crumbs, 1/2 cup sugar and butter in bowl. Press onto bottom and side of 10-inch springform pan sprayed with nonstick cooking spray. Bake at 325 degrees for 7 minutes. Cool. Cream 1 2/3 cups sugar and cream cheese in bowl until smooth. Add eggs 1 at a time, beating well after each addition. Stir in Bailey's Irish Cream, vanilla and 1/2 of the chocolate chips. Spoon into prepared crumb crust. Top with remaining chocolate chips. Bake at 325 degrees for 1 hour and 20 minutes. Cool in pan on wire rack. Remove from pan; place on serving plate. Beat whipping cream with 2 tablespoons sugar and coffee in mixer bowl until soft peaks form. Spread over top layer. Chill in refrigerator. Garnish with chocolate curls.

Approx Per Serving: Cal 901; Prot 13 g; Carbo 75 g; Fiber 1 g; T Fat 63 g; Chol 235 mg; Sod 491 mg.

Chocolate Almond Cheesecake

Yield: 12 servings Utensil: springform pan Preheat: 350 degrees

1½ cups graham cracker crumbs
3 tablespoons sugar
⅓ cup melted butter
1 cup sugar
16 ounces cream cheese, softened
⅛ teaspoon salt
2 teaspoons almond extract
3 eggs
8 ounces semisweet chocolate chips, melted
1 cup sour cream
2 tablespoons sugar
¾ teaspoon almond extract

Combine graham cracker crumbs, 3 tablespoons sugar and butter in small bowl; mix well. Press over side and bottom of 9-inch springform pan. Chill in refrigerator. Cream 1 cup sugar, cream cheese, salt and 2 teaspoons almond extract in mixer bowl until light and fluffy. Beat in eggs 1 at a time. Blend in chocolate. Pour into prepared pan. Bake at 350 degrees for 45 minutes. Do not open oven door. Turn off oven. Let stand in closed oven for 15 minutes. Cool in pan on wire rack. Chill for 2 hours. Blend sour cream, 2 tablespoons sugar and ¾ teaspoon almond extract in bowl. Chill in refrigerator. Place cheesecake on serving plate; remove side of pan. Top with sour cream mixture.

Approx Per Serving: Cal 481; Prot 7 g; Carbo 46 g; Fiber 1 g; T Fat 32 g; Chol 117 mg; Sod 299 mg.

Danish Puff

Yield: 16 servings Utensil: 2 jelly roll pans Preheat: 400 degrees

1 cup flour
¼ teaspoon salt
½ cup margarine, softened
2 tablespoons cold water
½ cup margarine
1 cup boiling water
1 teaspoon almond extract
1 cup flour
3 eggs
2 cups sifted confectioners' sugar
1 tablespoon butter
¼ cup half and half
1 teaspoon vanilla extract
⅛ teaspoon salt

Combine 1 cup flour and ¼ teaspoon salt in bowl. Cut in ½ cup margarine until crumbly. Add cold water; mix well. Divide into 2 portions. Shape into 3x12-inch rectangles. Place each rectangle on ungreased 10x15-inch jelly roll pan. Stir ½ cup margarine into boiling water in saucepan. Add almond extract. Remove from heat. Stir in remaining 1 cup flour. Beat in eggs 1 at a time. Spread over prepared pastry. Bake at 400 degrees for 30 minutes. Blend confectioners' sugar, butter, half and half, vanilla and ⅛ teaspoon salt in bowl. Spread over warm pastry. Cut into slices; serve warm.

Approx Per Serving: Cal 241; Prot 3 g; Carbo 25 g; Fiber <1 g; T Fat 15 g; Chol 47 mg; Sod 205 mg.

Frozen Lemon-Meringue Dessert

Yield: 24 servings Utensil: baking pan Preheat: broiler

2 cups crushed vanilla wafers
1/3 cup melted margarine
6 egg yolks
1 14-ounce can sweetened condensed milk
1 6-ounce can frozen lemonade concentrate, thawed
8 ounces whipped topping
6 egg whites
3/4 cup sugar

Mix vanilla wafers with melted margarine. Press into bottom of 9x13-inch baking pan. Beat egg yolks in mixer bowl until lemon-colored. Add condensed milk and lemonade concentrate, stirring until blended. Fold in whipped topping gently. Pour into prepared pan. Beat egg whites at medium speed in mixer bowl until soft peaks form. Add sugar gradually, beating constantly at high speed until stiff peaks form. Spread over filling, sealing to edge. Broil for 2 to 3 minutes or until meringue is lightly browned. Freeze until firm. Remove from freezer 10 to 15 minutes before serving.

Approx Per Serving: Cal 195; Prot 3 g; Carbo 26 g; Fiber <1 g; T Fat 9 g; Chol 64 mg; Sod 96 mg.

Fluffy Lemon Dessert

Yield: 24 servings Utensil: baking pan Preheat: no

60 round butter-flavored crackers, crushed
1/2 cup butter, softened
1/4 cup sugar
1 14-ounce can sweetened condensed milk
1 6-ounce can frozen lemonade concentrate, thawed
12 ounces whipped topping

Mix crushed crackers with butter and sugar in bowl. Reserve 1/4 cup crumb mixture for topping. Press remaining crumb mixture onto bottom of 9x13-inch baking pan. Mix condensed milk and lemonade concentrate together in bowl. Fold in whipped topping gently. Spread mixture over prepared crumb crust. Sprinkle with reserved cracker crumb mixture. Chill until firm before serving.

Approx Per Serving: Cal 381; Prot 4 g; Carbo 46 g; Fiber <1 g; T Fat 23 g; Chol 32 mg; Sod 264 mg.

Frozen Lemon Soufflé with Berry Sauce

Yield: 12 servings Utensil: soufflé dish Preheat: no

1½ cups sugar
1 cup plus 1 tablespoon lemon juice
1 cup unsalted butter, cut into pieces
14 egg yolks, lightly beaten
2 tablespoons grated lemon rind
3 egg whites
1½ cups whipping cream
1 10-ounce package frozen raspberries
¼ cup Crème de Cassis
½ cup whipping cream
1 tablespoon sugar
1 teaspoon vanilla extract
Candied Lemon Peel (see page 127)

Fold a 24-inch sheet of aluminum foil lengthwise into thirds. Brush one side with oil. Wrap foil, oiled side in, around top of 1½-quart soufflé dish, leaving a collar of 4 inches above edge of dish. Secure with string. Mix 1½ cups sugar, lemon juice, butter, egg yolks and lemon rind together in saucepan. Bring to a boil. Cook for 5 minutes or until thickened, stirring constantly. Do not overcook. Pour into bowl. Place bowl in larger bowl filled with ice and water. Cool completely, stirring frequently. Beat egg whites at medium speed in mixer bowl until soft peaks form. Fold into lemon mixture. Whip 1½ cups whipping cream in mixer bowl until soft peaks form. Fold gently into lemon mixture. Pour into prepared soufflé dish. Freeze overnight. Pureé raspberries in food processor. Strain through sieve into bowl. Stir in Crème de Cassis. Chill, covered, in refrigerator until serving time. Remove foil collar from soufflé dish. Return to freezer. Beat remaining ½ cup whipping cream with 1 tablespoon sugar and vanilla in mixer bowl at high speed until stiff peaks form. Spoon into pastry bag fitted with medium star tip. Pipe 8 rosettes around outer edge of soufflé. Sprinkle Candied Lemon Peel over each rosette. Serve with raspberry sauce. May substitute strawberries for raspberries.

Approx Per Serving: Cal 531; Prot 5 g; Carbo 45 g; Fiber 1 g; T Fat 38 g; Chol 344 mg; Sod 45 mg.

Pear Clafouti

Yield: 8 servings Utensil: pie plate Preheat: 350 degrees

1 29-ounce can pear halves, drained
4 eggs
1/3 cup sugar
1 1/2 cups milk
2 teaspoons vanilla extract
1 teaspoon grated lemon rind
1/4 teaspoon salt
3 English muffins, finely crumbled
1/2 cup butter
1 cup packed light brown sugar
1/2 cup whipping cream
1 teaspoon vanilla extract

Reserve 1 pear half for garnish. Cut into 8 slices; set aside. Chop remaining pears coarsely. Place in bottom of buttered 10-inch deep-dish pie plate. Beat eggs in bowl with sugar until thick and lemon-colored. Combine milk, 2 teaspoons vanilla, lemon rind and salt in bowl; mix well. Add to egg mixture. Stir in crumbled muffins. Pour mixture over pears. Bake at 350 degrees for 40 to 50 minutes or until set. Combine butter and brown sugar in saucepan. Cook over medium heat until butter is melted, stirring frequently. Add whipping cream gradually, stirring constantly. Bring just to the boiling point; remove from heat. Stir in remaining 1 teaspoon vanilla. Pour warm sauce into individual serving dishes. Add slice of clafouti. Garnish with whipped cream and reserved pear slice.

Approx Per Serving: Cal 488; Prot 7 g; Carbo 67 g; Fiber 2 g; T Fat 22 g; Chol 164 mg; Sod 382 mg.

Frozen Piña Colada Ice Cream Cake

Yield: 12 servings Utensil: springform pan Preheat: broiler

1 quart vanilla ice cream, softened
1 cup cream of coconut
1 8-ounce can crushed pineapple, drained
1/2 cup chopped walnuts
1 cup shredded sweetened coconut

Beat ice cream, cream of coconut, pineapple and walnuts in mixer bowl. Pour into 9-inch springform pan. Freeze, covered, overnight. Broil shredded coconut on baking sheet for 1 minute or until lightly browned. Let stand until cool. Remove cake from freezer; cut into wedges. Sprinkle each individual serving with toasted coconut.

Approx Per Serving: Cal 226; Prot 3 g; Carbo 18 g; Fiber 1 g; T Fat 17 g; Chol 20 mg; Sod 42 mg.

Praline Crêpes

Yield: 8 servings	Utensil: crêpe pan	Preheat: no

5 eggs, beaten
2 cups flour
2 tablespoons confectioners' sugar
1/8 teaspoon salt
2 cups milk
2 tablespoons brandy
1 tablespoon butter
5 apples, peeled, chopped
1/3 cup water
2 tablespoons sugar
1 teaspoon cinnamon
1/4 cup butter
1 cup packed light brown sugar
2 tablespoons light corn syrup
1/4 cup half and half
1 teaspoon vanilla extract
1/2 cup pecans
1 tablespoon brandy

Combine first 4 ingredients in large bowl; beat well. Add milk and 2 tablespoons brandy, stirring until smooth. Let stand for 30 minutes. Melt 1 tablespoon butter over medium heat in crêpe pan. Pour in 2 tablespoons of batter, spreading to cover bottom of pan. Brown on both sides. Remove to tray. Repeat process with remaining batter. Place crêpes on individual serving plates. Mix apples, water, sugar and cinnamon in medium saucepan. Bring to a boil, stirring frequently. Spoon mixture in center of each crêpe; fold over to cover filling. Mix 1/4 cup butter, brown sugar, corn syrup and half and half in small saucepan. Cook over low heat until butter melts, stirring constantly. Remove from heat. Add vanilla, pecans and 1 tablespoon brandy; mix well. Spoon sauce over crêpes. Garnish with whipped cream.

Approx Per Serving: Cal 510; Prot 10 g; Carbo 79 g; Fiber 3 g; T Fat 18 g; Chol 160 mg; Sod 469 mg.

Steamed Cranberry Pudding

Yield: 8 servings	Utensil: mold	Preheat: no

2 teaspoons soda
1/2 cup sorghum molasses
1/2 cup boiling water
1 1/3 cups sifted flour
1 teaspoon baking powder
1 cup fresh cranberries
1/4 cup flour
1/2 cup whipping cream
1/4 cup butter, softened
1/2 cup sugar

Add soda and molasses to boiling water in bowl; mix well. Sift flour with baking powder. Stir into molasses mixture. Toss cranberries with 1/4 cup flour to coat. Fold into batter. Pour into greased 1-quart mold; cover. Fill steamer with 1 to 2 inches water. Place mold in steamer. Steam for 2 hours. Turn pudding onto serving plate. Combine half and half, butter and sugar in top of double boiler; mix well. Cook for 15 minutes, stirring frequently. Pour warm sauce over pudding to serve. May double sauce recipe.

Approx Per Serving: Cal 289; Prot 3 g; Carbo 44 g; Fiber 1 g; T Fat 12 g; Chol 36 mg; Sod 320 mg.

IMMC Creamy Rice Pudding

Yield: 20 servings	Utensil: rice steamer	Preheat: no

7½ ounces long grain converted rice
2¼ cups plus ½ tablespoon water
¾ teaspoon salt
1½ cups milk (3.5% fat)
4¼ cups half and half
2⅓ teaspoons vanilla extract
2 tablespoons cornstarch
¾ cup sugar

Combine rice, water and salt in rice steamer. Steam for 30 minutes or until done. Place rice in large heavy saucepan. Add milk, half and half and vanilla; mix well. Mix cornstarch and sugar together. Stir into rice mixture. Bring to the boiling point. Simmer for 15 minutes or until of desired consistency, stirring constantly. Chill in refrigerator. Garnish with whipped cream and sprinkle of cinnamon.

Approx Per Serving: Cal 289; Prot 6 g; Carbo 25 g; Fiber <1 g; T Fat 18 g; Chol 64 mg; Sod 152 mg.

IMMC Tropical Rice Pudding

Yield: 25 servings	Utensil: rice steamer	Preheat: no

13 ounces long-grain converted rice
5 cups water
1½ cups pineapple tidbits, drained
1½ cups mandarin oranges, drained
6¾ cups prepared low-calorie pineapple whipped topping
25 mandarin orange slices

Combine rice and water in rice steamer. Steam, uncovered, for 40 minutes, stirring occasionally. Rice will be soupy; do not drain. Chill, covered, overnight. Stir pineapple and 1½ cups mandarin oranges into rice. Fold in whipped topping. Spoon into individual serving bowls. Top with mandarin orange slices.

Approx Per Serving: Cal 122; Prot 2 g; Carbo 23 g; Fiber <1 g; T Fat 3 g; Chol 4 mg; Sod 8 mg.

Refrigerator Strawberry Dessert

Yield: 12 servings   Utensil: dish   Preheat: no

1 8-ounce package vanilla wafers, crushed
1/2 cup margarine, softened
1 1/2 cups confectioners' sugar
2 eggs, beaten
1 quart fresh strawberries, sliced
1 cup sweetened whipped cream

Line bottom of 8x11-inch dish with half the vanilla wafer crumbs. Cream margarine and confectioners' sugar in mixer bowl until light and fluffy. Add eggs, beating until smooth and creamy. Spread mixture carefully over crumbs. Layer with strawberries and whipped cream. Sprinkle remaining crumbs over top. Chill for 3 hours or longer before serving.

Approx Per Serving: Cal 283; Prot 3 g; Carbo 35 g; Fiber 1 g; T Fat 16 g; Chol 61 mg; Sod 176 mg.

Yummy Dessert

Yield: 15 servings   Utensil: baking pan   Preheat: 350 degrees

1 cup flour
1/4 cup packed brown sugar
1/2 cup margarine, softened
1/2 cup finely chopped pecans
1/2 teaspoons almond or vanilla extract
1 cup confectioners' sugar
8 ounces cream cheese
1 21-ounce can cherry pie filling
12 ounces creamy whipped topping

Combine flour, brown sugar, margarine and pecans in bowl; mix well. Press into 9x13-inch baking pan; mix well. Bake at 350 degrees for 15 to 20 minutes or until lightly browned, stirring occasionally. Reserve 1/2 cup of mixture for topping. Press remaining mixture onto bottom of pan. Chill in refrigerator. Cream almond extract, confectioners' sugar and cream cheese in bowl until light and fluffy. Spread over cooled crust. Layer with pie filling and whipped topping. Sprinkle with reserved crumb mixture. Chill for several hours or until firm. May substitute fresh strawberries for cherry pie filling.

Approx Per Serving: Cal 318; Prot 3 g; Carbo 34 g; Fiber 1 g; T Fat 20 g; Chol 17 mg; Sod 136 mg.

ALMOND BARK CANDY

Yield: 100 servings   Utensil: ovenproof bowl   Preheat: 200 degrees

2 pounds butterscotch bark, chopped
1 cup chunky peanut butter
2 cups miniature marshmallows
2 cups chopped dry roasted peanuts
5 cups crisp rice cereal

Place bark in large ovenproof bowl. Bake at 200 degrees for 20 minutes or until melted. Stir in peanut butter. Add marshmallows, peanuts and cereal, stirring until coated. Drop by teaspoonfuls onto waxed paper. Cool.

Approx Per Serving: Cal 87; Prot 2 g; Carbo 8 g; Fiber 1 g; T Fat 6 g; Chol 0 mg; Sod 30 mg.

NEVER FAIL DIVINITY

Yield: 64 servings   Utensil: square pan   Preheat: no

2 cups sugar
1/2 cup water
1/8 teaspoon salt
1 7-ounce jar marshmallow creme
1/2 cup chopped pecans
1 teaspoon vanilla extract

Combine sugar, water and salt in saucepan. Cook over medium heat to 250 degrees on candy thermometer, hard-ball stage. Place marshmallow creme in bowl; stir in hot liquid. Beat until slightly stiff. Fold in pecans and vanilla. Spoon into buttered 9-inch square pan. Cut into squares.

Approx Per Serving: Cal 57; Prot <1 g; Carbo 13 g; Fiber <1 g; T Fat 1 g; Chol 0 mg; Sod 9 mg.

CHEESE FUDGE

Yield: 72 servings   Utensil: shallow dish   Preheat: no

2 cups butter
1 pound American cheese, shredded
4 1-pound packages confectioners' sugar
1 cup baking cocoa
1 tablespoon vanilla extract
1 cup chopped pecans

Place butter and cheese in large saucepan. Cook over low heat until both are melted, stirring frequently. Remove from heat. Sift confectioners' sugar and cocoa together. Stir into melted cheese mixture. Add vanilla and pecans; mix well. Pour into buttered 9x13-inch dish. Store in refrigerator.

Approx Per Serving: Cal 200; Prot 2 g; Carbo 31 g; Fiber <1 g; T Fat 8 g; Chol 20 mg; Sod 134 mg.

Bob's Favorite Candy

Yield: 36 servings   Utensil: double boiler   Preheat: no

8 ounces white bark
2 cups chocolate chips
1 pound salted peanuts

Melt bark and chocolate chips in double boiler, stirring frequently. Remove from heat. Stir in peanuts. Drop by teaspoonfuls onto waxed paper-covered tray.

Approx Per Serving: Cal 153; Prot 4 g; Carbo 11 g; Fiber 2 g; T Fat 12 g; Chol 0 mg; Sod 57 mg.

Candied Lemon Peel

Yield: 1 serving   Utensil: saucepan   Preheat: no

2 large lemons
1/4 cup sugar
1/2 cup water
1/4 cup sugar

Remove lemon peel in large strips with vegetable peeler. Cut into julienne strips. Blanch in boiling water in small saucepan for 1 minute; drain. Repeat blanching and draining. Bring 1/4 cup sugar and water to a boil over low heat in small heavy saucepan, stirring until sugar dissolves. Add lemon peel. Simmer for 15 minutes, stirring frequently; drain. Toss with remaining 1/4 cup sugar to coat. Place on plate. Let stand for 30 minutes or until dry. Store between sheets of waxed paper in airtight container. Do not refrigerate.

Approx Per Serving: Cal 419; Prot 1 g; Carbo 110 g; Fiber 2 g; T Fat <1 g; Chol 0 mg; Sod 5 mg.

Easy Peanut Brittle

Yield: 20 servings   Utensil: metal tray   Preheat: no

1 cup light corn syrup
1 cup sugar
1 tablespoon margarine
1/4 teaspoon salt
1 pound raw Spanish peanuts
1 teaspoon soda

Combine first 4 ingredients in saucepan. Cook over medium heat until sugar dissolves, stirring constantly. Add peanuts. Cook for 20 minutes longer, stirring constantly. Remove from heat. Stir in soda. Spread onto greased tray. Cool until set. Break into pieces.

Approx Per Serving: Cal 221; Prot 6 g; Carbo 26 g; Fiber 2 g; T Fat 12 g; Chol 0 mg; Sod 139 mg.

IMMC Peanut Butter Candy

Yield: 35 servings Utensil: large dish Preheat: no

2 cups melted margarine
3 cups creamy peanut butter
2 1-pound packages confectioners' sugar
13½ ounces graham cracker crumbs
4 cups semisweet chocolate chips

Combine margarine, peanut butter, confectioners' sugar and graham cracker crumbs in large bowl; mix well. Press into greased dish. Chill until set. Melt chocolate chips in double boiler. Spread over peanut butter mixture evenly. Chill before serving. Cut into 35 squares.

Approx Per Serving: Cal 896; Prot 11 g; Carbo 91 g; Fiber 2 g; T Fat 64 g; Chol 0 mg; Sod 307 mg.

Toffee Clusters

Yield: 40 servings Utensil: glass bowl MW

1 pound almond bark
2 cups chocolate chips
1 10-ounce package butter brickle chips

Place almond bark in glass bowl. Microwave for 5 minutes or until almond bark melts, stirring with wooden spoon frequently. Add chocolate chips. Microwave for 1 to 1½ minutes or until melted. Stir in butter brickle chips. Drop by teaspoonfuls onto waxed paper-lined tray.

Approx Per Serving: Cal 139; Prot 1 g; Carbo 13 g; Fiber 1 g; T Fat 11 g; Chol 0 mg; Sod 19 mg.

Chinese Almond Cookies

Yield: 36 servings Utensil: cookie sheet Preheat: 300 degrees

1 teaspoon almond extract
2 cups shortening
4 cups flour
1½ cups sugar
1½ teaspoons salt
¾ cup whole blanched almonds

Cream almond extract and shortening in mixer bowl until smooth. Add flour gradually, mixing well after each addition. Add sugar and salt. Knead until paste is formed. Shape into thick roll; cut into ½-inch slices. Place on ungreased cookie sheet. Press almond into center of each cookie. Bake at 300 degrees for 30 minutes. May subsitute butter or margarine for shortening.

Approx Per Serving: Cal 201; Prot 2 g; Carbo 19 g; Fiber 1 g; T Fat 13 g; Chol 0 mg; Sod 90 mg.

Apple Pie Bars

Yield: 56 servings Utensil: cookie sheet Preheat: 425 degrees

2½ cups flour
¾ teaspoon salt
1 cup shortening
½ cup (about) milk
1 egg yolk
6 cups peeled, sliced Jonathan apples
1⅓ cups sugar
½ teaspoon cinnamon
2 tablespoons flour
¼ cup tapioca
1 egg white, beaten until foamy
1 cup confectioners' sugar
2 tablespoons milk
Almond or vanilla extract to taste

Blend 2½ cups flour and salt in bowl. Cut in shortening until crumbly. Add enough milk to egg yolk to equal ⅔ cup liquid. Add to flour mixture, mixing with fork until ball is formed. Divide into 2 portions. Roll each portion of dough to size of cookie sheet. Place 1 portion of dough on cookie sheet; cover with apples. Sprinkle with mixture of sugar, cinnamon, 2 tablespoons flour and tapioca. Top with remaining portion of dough; seal edges. Brush egg white over top. Bake at 425 degrees for 10 minutes. Reduce temperature to 375 degrees. Bake for 30 minutes longer. Glaze with mixture of remaining ingredients. Cut into 2x2-inch bars.

Approx Per Serving: Cal 93; Prot 1 g; Carbo 14 g; Fiber <1 g; T Fat 4 g; Chol 4 mg; Sod 31 mg.

Best Brownies

Yield: 20 servings Utensil: baking pan Preheat: 350 degrees

½ cup margarine, softened
1 cup sugar
4 eggs
1 teaspoon vanilla extract
1 16-ounce can chocolate syrup
1 cup plus 1 tablespoon flour
½ cup chopped pecans
½ teaspoon baking powder
6 tablespoons butter
6 tablespoons milk
1½ cups sugar
1 cup chocolate chips
½ cup chopped pecans

Cream margarine and 1 cup sugar in bowl until light and fluffy. Add eggs; mix well. Add vanilla, chocolate syrup, flour, pecans and baking powder; mix well. Spread into greased 10x15-inch baking pan. Bake at 350 degrees for 30 minutes. Combine butter, milk and remaining 1½ cups sugar in saucepan. Bring to a full rolling boil for 30 seconds. Add chocolate chips and pecans; mix well. Cool slightly. Spread over brownies.

Approx Per Serving: Cal 345; Prot 4 g; Carbo 50 g; Fiber 1 g; T Fat 17 g; Chol 53 mg; Sod 127 mg.

CANDIED FRUIT BROWNIES

Yield: 36 servings   Utensil: baking pan   Preheat: 375 degrees

4 eggs
2 cups packed light
  brown sugar
1 tablespoon cold water
2 cups flour
1 cup chopped candied
  fruit
1 teaspoon cinnamon
¼ teaspoon salt
1 cup pecans

Beat eggs in bowl until very light. Add brown sugar and water; beat well. Mix flour, fruit and cinnamon in medium bowl. Add salt and pecans. Add to egg mixture. Spoon into greased 9x13-inch baking pan. Bake at 375 degrees for 20 minutes.

Approx Per Serving: Cal 122; Prot 2 g; Carbo 23 g; Fiber <1 g; T Fat 3 g; Chol 24 mg; Sod 28 mg.

IMMC BROWNIES WITH WALNUTS

Yield: 35 servings   Utensil: baking pan   Preheat: 350 degrees

1¼ cups margarine,
  softened
2½ cups sugar
5 eggs
6 ounces chocolate naps,
  melted
2½ cups all-purpose flour
½ teaspoon salt
1 cup chopped walnuts
2 cups chocolate frosting

Cream margarine and sugar in mixer bowl until light and fluffy. Add eggs. Beat until creamy. Add chocolate naps; mix well. Add flour, salt and walnuts; mix well. Pour into greased 9x12-inch baking pan. Bake at 350 degrees for about 20 minutes or until brownies test done. Frost with chocolate frosting. Note: May make white frosting by creaming 7 teaspoons softened margarine, ¼ cup plus 1 teaspoon shortening and adding 2 cups plus 5 tablespoons confectioners' sugar, 6½ teaspoons milk and vanilla to taste. Tint with 2 to 4 drops of food coloring. May tint green and add ¼ teaspoon mint extract.

Approx Per Serving: Cal 413; Prot 4 g; Carbo 67 g; Fiber 1 g; T Fat 17 g; Chol 39 mg; Sod 148 mg.

Prize-Winning Hunka Chocolate Cookies

Yield: 60 servings Utensil: cookie sheet Preheat: 350 degrees

2 cups semisweet chocolate chips
4 ounces unsweetened chocolate
1/4 cup margarine
4 eggs
1 1/3 cups sugar
2 teaspoons vanilla extract
1/2 cup flour
1/2 teaspoon baking powder
2 cups semisweet chocolate chips
2 to 3 cups toasted walnut pieces

Place 2 cups chocolate chips, unsweetened chocolate and margarine in saucepan. Cook over low heat until melted, stirring constantly. Pour into large mixer bowl. Add eggs, sugar and vanilla; mix well. Sift in flour and baking powder, mixing at low speed until blended. Stir in remaining 2 cups chocolate chips and walnuts. Drop by heaping teaspoonfuls onto greased cookie sheet; flatten slightly. Bake at 350 degrees for 10 minutes or until edges are firm and surface is dull and cracked. Cool on cookie sheet for 2 minutes. Remove to wire rack to cool completely. Garnish by drizzling with melted white chocolate and semisweet chocolate.

Approx Per Serving: Cal 138; Prot 2 g; Carbo 13 g; Fiber 1 g; T Fat 10 g; Chol 14 mg; Sod 19 mg.

IMMC Chocolate Chip Cookies

Yield: 50 servings Utensil: cookie sheet Preheat: 350 degrees

1 cup packed brown sugar
1 cup sugar
1 cup shortening
3 eggs
1/2 cup half and half
4 1/2 cups flour
1 1/2 teaspoons salt
2 teaspoons soda
1 cup chopped walnuts
2 cups semisweet chocolate chips
1 teaspoon vanilla extract

Cream brown sugar, sugar and shortening in bowl until light and fluffy. Add eggs and half and half; mix well. Sift flour, salt and soda into creamed mixture; mix well. Stir in walnuts, chocolate chips and vanilla. Shape by 2 generous tablespoonfuls into balls. Place on cookie sheet. Bake at 350 degrees for 12 to 15 minutes. Cool on cookie sheet for 2 minutes. Remove to wire rack to cool completely.

Approx Per Serving: Cal 419; Prot 4 g; Carbo 49 g; Fiber 1 g; T Fat 27 g; Chol 22 mg; Sod 123 mg.

Famous Chocolate Chip Cookies

Yield: 60 servings   Utensil: cookie sheet   Preheat: 375 degrees

5 cups oats
4 cups flour
1 teaspoon salt
2 teaspoons baking powder
2 teaspoons soda
2 cups butter, softened
2 cups sugar
2 cups packed brown sugar
4 eggs
2 teaspoons vanilla extract
4 cups chocolate chips
1 8-ounce chocolate candy bar, finely grated

Place 1 cup oats in blender container. Process until pulverized. Combine with remaining 4 cups oats, flour, salt, baking powder and soda in bowl; mix well. Cream butter, sugar and brown sugar in large mixer bowl until light and creamy. Add eggs and vanilla; mix well. Add flour mixture to creamed mixture; mix well. Stir in chocolate chips and grated chocolate. Shape into 2-inch balls. Place 2 inches apart on ungreased cookie sheets. Bake at 375 degrees for 6 to 8 minutes or until golden brown. Remove to wire rack to cool.

Approx Per Serving: Cal 246; Prot 3 g; Carbo 33 g; Fiber 1 g; T Fat 12 g; Chol 32 mg; Sod 138 mg.

Coconut-Walnut Shortbread Bars

Yield: 100 servings   Utensil: baking pan   Preheat: 275 degrees

3 cups butter, softened
1¾ cups confectioners' sugar
4 cups plus 2 tablespoons flour
4 teaspoons cornstarch
7 eggs
3 cups packed light brown sugar
1 tablespoon vanilla extract
1 tablespoon light corn syrup
5½ cups chopped walnuts
¾ cup plus 2 tablespoons flaked coconut
1 egg
1 teaspoon water

Cream butter and 1¾ cups confectioners' sugar in mixer bowl until light and fluffy. Blend in flour and cornstarch. Press into bottom of 12x17-inch baking pan. Prick with fork. Bake at 275 degrees for 1 hour and 10 minutes or until golden brown. Beat 7 eggs, brown sugar, vanilla and corn syrup in large bowl. Stir in walnuts and coconut. Brush baked shortbread with mixture of remaining 1 egg and water. Spread walnut mixture over top evenly. Increase oven temperature to 350 degrees. Bake for 25 minutes or until top is golden brown and set. Cool completely. Cut into 1x2-inch bars. Store in airtight container.

Approx Per Serving: Cal 153; Prot 2 g; Carbo 14 g; Fiber 1 g; T Fat 10 g; Chol 32 mg; Sod 56 mg.

IMMC Glazed Lemon Bars

Yield: 35 servings   Utensil: baking pan   Preheat: 375 degrees

1¼ cups margarine, softened
3 cups all-purpose flour
¼ cup plus 2 tablespoons confectioners' sugar
½ cup lemon juice
13 ounces frozen egg or egg substitute
3½ cups sugar
¾ cup all-purpose flour
1 tablespoon baking powder
2 cups confectioners' sugar
1 tablespoon plus 1½ teaspoons lemon juice
¼ cup water

Combine margarine, 3 cups flour and ¼ cup plus 2 tablespoons confectioners' sugar in bowl, mixing just until crumbly. Pat firmly into greased 10x15-inch baking pan. Bake at 375 degrees for 10 minutes. Combine ½ cup lemon juice, eggs, sugar, remaining ¾ cup flour and baking powder in large bowl. Whisk until mixture begins to thicken. Pour over baked crust. Bake for 20 to 25 minutes longer. Cool to room temperature. Combine remaining 2 cups confectioners' sugar, 1 tablespoon plus 1½ teaspoons lemon juice and water in small bowl; mix well. Spread over baked layer thinly. Cut into bars.

Approx Per Serving: Cal 282; Prot 3 g; Carbo 51 g; Fiber <1 g; T Fat 8 g; Chol 58 mg; Sod 134 mg.

Oatmeal Caramel Bars

Yield: 36 servings   Utensil: baking pan   Preheat: 325 degrees

1 cup melted butter
½ teaspoon salt
¾ teaspoon soda
1½ cups flour
1½ cups oats
40 caramels
5 tablespoons milk
1¼ cups chocolate chips
1 cup chopped walnuts

Mix butter, salt, soda, flour and oats in greased 9x13-inch baking pan. Reserve half the crumb mixture for topping. Press remaining crumb mixture into bottom of pan. Bake at 325 degrees for 10 minutes. Place caramels and milk in glass bowl. Microwave on High until melted, stirring twice. Sprinkle chocolate chips over baked crust. Let stand until chocolate melts; spread over crust. Drizzle with melted caramels. Sprinkle with walnuts; top with reserved crumb mixture. Bake for 15 minutes longer. Cool. Cut into bars.

Approx Per Serving: Cal 181; Prot 2 g; Carbo 20 g; Fiber 1 g; T Fat 11 g; Chol 15 mg; Sod 120 mg.

Whole Wheat Molasses Sugar Cookies

Yield: 48 servings   Utensil: cookie sheet   Preheat: 375 degrees

3/4 cup margarine, softened
1 cup sugar
1/4 cup molasses
1 egg
1 cup all-purpose flour
1 cup whole wheat flour
2 teaspoons soda
1 teaspoon cinnamon
1/2 teaspoon ground cloves
1/2 teaspoon light salt
1 cup (about) sugar

Cream margarine and 1 cup sugar in mixer bowl until light and fluffy. Add molasses and egg; mix well. Sift in all-purpose flour, whole wheat flour, soda, cinnamon, cloves and salt; mix well. Cover bowl. Chill for 1 to 3 hours. Shape into 1-inch balls; roll in remaining sugar. Place on cookie sheet. Bake at 375 degrees for 8 to 10 minutes or until golden brown. Cool on wire rack.

Approx Per Serving: Cal 81; Prot 1 g; Carbo 13 g; Fiber <1 g; T Fat 3 g; Chol 4 mg; Sod 83 mg.

Pumpkin Bars

Yield: 48 servings   Utensil: baking pan   Preheat: 350 degrees

2 cups flour
2 cups sugar
2 teaspoons baking powder
1 teaspoon soda
1/4 teaspoon salt
2 teaspoons cinnamon
1 teaspoon pumpkin pie spice
1 16-ounce can pumpkin
1 cup salad oil
4 eggs
Pumpkin Bar Frosting

Combine flour, sugar, baking powder, soda, salt, cinnamon, pumpkin pie spice, pumpkin, oil and eggs in large bowl; mix well. Pour into lightly greased 11x16-inch baking pan. Bake at 350 degrees for 20 to 25 minutes or until top springs back when touched. Top with Pumpkin Bar Frosting when partially cooled.

Pumpkin Bar Frosting

3 ounces cream cheese, softened
6 tablespoons melted butter
1 teaspoon milk
1 teaspoon vanilla extract
2 cups confectioners' sugar

Combine cream cheese, butter, milk, vanilla and confectioners' sugar in mixer bowl. Beat until smooth. May substitute margarine and water for butter and milk.

Approx Per Serving: Cal 139; Prot 1 g; Carbo 18 g; Fiber <1 g; T Fat 7 g; Chol 24 mg; Sod 66 mg.

Cakes and Pies

Fresh Apple Cake with Hot Sauce

Yield: 8 servings　　　Utensil: cake pan　　　Preheat: 350 degrees

1/4 cup shortening
1 cup sugar
1 egg, beaten
3 apples, peeled, grated
1 teaspoon soda
1/4 teaspoon salt
1 cup flour
1/2 teaspoon cinnamon
1/4 cup chopped pecans
1/2 cup butter
1/2 cup half and half
1 cup sugar
1 1/2 teaspoons vanilla extract

Cream shortening and sugar together in bowl until light and fluffy. Add egg and apples, beating well. Sift together soda, salt, flour and cinnamon. Add to creamed mixture with walnuts; beat well. Pour into greased 8x8-inch cake pan. Bake at 350 degrees for 45 minutes or until cake tests done. Cool in pan for 5 minutes. Invert onto serving plate. Combine butter, half and half, sugar and vanilla in top of double boiler. Cook until mixture is thickened, stirring occasionally. Pour over warm cake.

Approx Per Serving: Cal 509; Prot 3 g; Carbo 75 g; Fiber 3 g; T Fat 23 g; Chol 63 mg; Sod 283 mg.

Jewish Apple Cake

Yield: 15 servings　　　Utensil: bundt pan　　　Preheat: 325 degrees

4 eggs
2 cups sugar
1 cup vegetable oil
1/4 cup orange juice
2 1/2 teaspoons vanilla extract
3 cups flour
1/2 teaspoon salt
1 tablespoon baking powder
1 cup chopped pecans
1 tablespoon sugar
1 teaspoon cinnamon
2 cups thinly sliced apples

Beat eggs, sugar, oil, orange juice and vanilla in large bowl. Sift flour, salt and baking powder into mixture. Stir in walnuts. Combine 1 tablespoon sugar with cinnamon. Sprinkle over sliced apples. Pour 1/3 of the batter into well greased bundt pan. Arrange 1/2 of the apples over batter. Repeat layers, ending with batter. Bake at 325 degrees for 1 hour. Cool in pan for 10 minutes. Invert onto serving plate; garnish with confectioners' sugar.

Approx Per Serving: Cal 403; Prot 5 g; Carbo 49 g; Fiber 2 g; T Fat 22 g; Chol 57 mg; Sod 157 mg.

Apricot Brandy Cake

Yield: 16 servings Utensil: bundt pan Preheat: 325 degrees

½ cup chopped pecans
1 2-layer package yellow cake mix
1 4-ounce package vanilla instant pudding mix
½ cup apricot brandy
½ cup water
½ cup oil
4 eggs, beaten
½ cup water
1 cup sugar
½ cup butter

Sprinkle pecans in bottom of greased and floured bundt pan. Combine cake mix and pudding mix in mixer bowl. Add brandy, ½ cup water, oil and eggs. Beat at medium speed for 2 minutes. Pour into prepared bundt pan. Bake at 325 degrees for 50 to 60 minutes. Combine remaining ½ cup water, sugar and butter in saucepan. Boil for 2 to 3 minutes, stirring constantly. Pour immediately over warm cake. Cool cake for 30 minutes in pan. Remove to serving plate. Allow to "ripen" for several days.

Approx Per Serving: Cal 382; Prot 3 g; Carbo 49 g; Fiber <1 g; T Fat 19 g; Chol 69 mg; Sod 307 mg.

Carrot Cake

Yield: 20 servings Utensil: cake pan Preheat: 350 degrees

4 eggs, well beaten
2 cups sugar
1½ cups oil
2 cups flour
2 teaspoons soda
1 teaspoon cinnamon
3 4-ounce jars strained baby food carrots
¼ cup margarine, softened
8 ounces cream cheese, softened
2 cups confectioners' sugar
½ teaspoon vanilla extract

Combine eggs, sugar, oil, flour, soda and cinnamon in large bowl; mix well. Add carrots, stirring until blended. Pour into greased 9x12-inch cake pan. Bake at 350 degrees for 25 to 30 minutes or until cake tests done. Cool in pan for 10 minutes. Remove to wire rack to cool completely. Cream margarine, cream cheese, confectioners' sugar and vanilla until light and fluffy. Spread frosting over cooled cake.

Approx Per Serving: Cal 389; Prot 3 g; Carbo 42 g; Fiber <1 g; T Fat 24 g; Chol 55 mg; Sod 157 mg.

Easy Carrot Cake

Yield: 15 servings   Utensil: cake pan   Preheat: 350 degrees

1 2-layer package yellow cake mix
1¼ cups mayonnaise-type salad dressing
4 eggs
1⅓ cups water
2 teaspoons cinnamon
2 cups shredded carrots
½ cup chopped pecans
3 ounces cream cheese, softened
1 tablespoon milk
½ teaspoon vanilla extract
3 cups confectioners' sugar

Combine cake mix, salad dressing, eggs, water and cinnamon in mixer bowl; beat until well mixed. Stir in carrots and pecans. Pour into greased 9x13-inch cake pan. Bake at 350 degrees for 35 minutes or until cake tests done. Let stand until cool. Combine cream cheese, milk, vanilla and confectioners' sugar in mixer bowl; beat until creamy. Spread over cooled cake.

Approx Per Serving: Cal 389; Prot 4 g; Carbo 60 g; Fiber 1 g; T Fat 16 g; Chol 68 mg; Sod 390 mg.

Low-Cholesterol Chocolate Cake

Yield: 12 servings   Utensil: baking pan   Preheat: 350 degrees

2 cups flour
1¾ cups sugar
½ cup baking cocoa
½ teaspoon salt
1 tablespoon soda
⅔ cup corn oil
1 cup buttermilk
1 cup hot strong coffee
3 tablespoons baking cocoa
1 cup sugar
⅓ cup milk
¼ cup margarine
½ teaspoon salt
1 teaspoon vanilla extract

Sift flour, 1¾ cups sugar, ½ cup cocoa, ½ teaspoon salt and soda into large bowl. Add oil and buttermilk, stirring until blended. Add coffee, stirring gently. Pour mixture into greased and floured 9x13-inch cake pan. Bake at 350 degrees for 35 to 40 minutes. Cool on wire rack. Turn onto serving plate. Combine 3 tablespoons cocoa, 1 cup sugar, milk, margarine and ½ teaspoon salt in saucepan; mix well. Bring to a boil. Cook for 1 minute, stirring constantly. Remove from heat. Stir in vanilla. Cook for 15 to 30 minutes or until mixture is thick enough to spread, stirring constantly. Frost cooled cake.

Approx Per Serving: Cal 419; Prot 4 g; Carbo 65 g; Fiber 2 g; T Fat 18 g; Chol 2 mg; Sod 455 mg.

Wacky Chocolate Delight

Yield: 12 servings Utensil: cake pan Preheat: 375 degrees

1½ cups all-purpose flour
1 cup sugar
⅓ cup baking cocoa
1 teaspoon soda
½ teaspoon salt
1 tablespoon vanilla extract
1 tablespoon cider vinegar
½ cup vegetable oil
1 cup water
1 tablespoon confectioners' sugar

Combine flour, sugar, cocoa, soda and salt in bowl; mix well. Make well in center of mixture. Add vanilla, vinegar and oil. Stir in water gradually until blended. Pour into greased 8x8-inch cake pan. Bake at 375 degrees for 25 to 30 minutes or until cake tests done. Do not overbake. Cool in pan for 10 minutes. Remove to wire rack to cool completely. Turn onto serving plate. Sift confectioners' sugar over top of cake.

Approx Per Serving: Cal 175; Prot 2 g; Carbo 29 g; Fiber 1 g; T Fat 6 g; Chol 0 mg; Sod 158 mg.

Delicate Cake

Yield: 10 servings Utensil: 2 cake pans Preheat: 350 degrees

1 cup margarine, softened
½ cup sugar
4 egg yolks
¼ cup milk
¾ cup flour
1 teaspoon baking powder
1 teaspoon vanilla extract
4 egg whites
1 cup sugar
½ cup crushed pecans
2 teaspoons cinnamon
1 cup whipping cream, whipped
2 cups fresh strawberries

Cream margarine and ½ cup sugar in bowl until light and fluffy. Stir in egg yolks and milk. Add flour, baking powder and vanilla extract; mix well. Pour into two 9x9-inch cake pans. Beat egg whites in mixer bowl until soft peaks form. Add 1 cup sugar gradually, beating constantly at high speed until stiff peaks form. Spread over each layer. Sprinkle ½ cup crushed pecans and 1 teaspoon cinnamon over each layer. Bake at 350 degrees for 25 minutes. Cool on wire rack. Invert one layer onto serving plate. Spread with mixture of whipped cream and strawberries. Place second layer on top, meringue side up.

Approx Per Serving: Cal 482; Prot 5 g; Carbo 42 g; Fiber 2 g; T Fat 34 g; Chol 119 mg; Sod 283 mg.

Depression Cake

Yield: 12 servings   Utensil: cake pan   Preheat: 350 degrees

2 cups packed light brown sugar
2 tablespoons shortening
1 cup raisins
1 teaspoon ground cloves
1 teaspoon salt
1 teaspoon cinnamon
2 cups hot water
1 teaspoon soda
1 teaspoon water
1/2 cup pecan pieces
2 cups flour

Combine sugar, shortening, raisins, cloves, salt and cinnamon with hot water in saucepan. Bring to a boil. Cook for 5 minutes, stirring constantly. Cool. Add mixture of soda and water. Add pecan pieces to flour; toss well. Stir into mixture. Pour into greased 9x13-inch cake pan. Bake at 350 degrees for 25 minutes or until cake tests done. Cool on wire rack. Turn onto serving plate.

Approx Per Serving: Cal 306; Prot 3 g; Carbo 63 g; Fiber 2 g; T Fat 6 g; Chol 0 mg; Sod 264 mg.

Heath Bar Cake

Yield: 15 servings   Utensil: cake pan   Preheat: 350 degrees

1 2-layer package German Chocolate cake mix
1/2 14-ounce can sweetened condensed milk
1/2 cup (or more) caramel-fudge topping
12 ounces whipped topping
3 Heath bars, crushed

Prepare and bake cake using package directions for 9x13-inch cake pan. Make 32 holes in cake with handle of wooden spoon. Pour sweetened condensed milk and caramel-fudge topping over cake. Top with whipped topping. Sprinkle Heath bars over topping. Chill until serving time.

Approx Per Serving: Cal 422; Prot 8 g; Carbo 51 g; Fiber <1 g; T Fat 22 g; Chol 33 mg; Sod 280 mg.

Lemon Cake

Yield: 16 servings Utensil: cake pan Preheat: 350 degrees

1 3-ounce package lemon gelatin
3/4 cup water
4 eggs
1 2-layer package lemon cake mix
3/4 cup vegetable oil
2 cups confectioners' sugar
1/2 cup lemon juice

Beat gelatin, water and eggs together in mixer bowl. Add cake mix. Beat for 3 to 4 minutes or until smooth. Beat in oil. Pour into 9x13-inch greased cake pan. Bake at 350 degrees for 30 minutes or until cake tests done. Combine confectioners' sugar with lemon juice; beat until smooth. Prick top of cake with fork. Pour glaze over top. Return to oven. Bake for 10 minutes longer. Cool on wire rack. Turn onto serving plate.

Approx Per Serving: Cal 326; Prot 3 g; Carbo 47 g; Fiber <1 g; T Fat 14 g; Chol 53 mg; Sod 231 mg.

Aunt Ellen's Oatmeal Cake

Yield: 20 servings Utensil: cake pan Preheat: 350 degrees

1 cup oats
1/2 cup butter, softened
1 1/4 cups boiling water
1 cup sugar
1 cup packed brown sugar
2 eggs, beaten
1/2 teaspoon salt
1 teaspoon cinnamon
1/2 teaspoon nutmeg
1 teaspoon soda
1 1/3 cups flour
1/2 cup butter, softened
1/4 cup evaporated milk
1/2 cup sugar
1 teaspoon vanilla extract
1 cup shredded coconut
1 cup pecan pieces

Combine oats, 1/2 cup butter and boiling water in small bowl; mix well. Let stand for 20 minutes. Beat sugars, eggs, salt, cinnamon, nutmeg and soda together in large bowl. Add flour, stirring to blend in. Stir in oat mixture. Pour into greased and floured 9x13-inch cake pan. Bake at 350 degrees for 30 to 45 minutes or until cake tests done. Cool in pan on wire rack. Combine remaining 1/2 cup butter, evaporated milk, remaining 1/2 cup sugar, vanilla, coconut and pecans in bowl; mix well. Spread over cooled cake. Broil for about 5 minutes or until coconut is lightly browned. Serve with whipped cream if desired.

Approx Per Serving: Cal 295; Prot 3 g; Carbo 38 g; Fiber 2 g; T Fat 16 g; Chol 47 mg; Sod 188 mg.

Pineapple Cake with Icing

Yield: 12 servings   Utensil: cake pan   Preheat: 350 degrees

2 eggs, beaten
2 cups sugar
¼ cup vegetable oil
1 teaspoon vanilla extract
½ teaspoon salt
2 cups flour
2 teaspoons soda
1 20-ounce can crushed pineapple
½ cup margarine
8 ounces cream cheese, softened
1 teaspoon vanilla extract
1 1-pound package confectioners' sugar

Combine eggs, sugar, oil, vanilla and salt in large bowl; mix well. Sift together flour and soda; add to mixture. Stir in undrained pineapple. Pour into greased and floured 9x13-inch cake pan. Bake at 350 degrees for 40 minutes or until cake tests done. Cool in pan for 5 minutes. Turn onto serving plate. Cream margarine, cream cheese, vanilla and confectioners' sugar together in bowl until light and fluffy. Spread over warm cake.

Approx Per Serving: Cal 577; Prot 5 g; Carbo 98 g; Fiber 1 g; T Fat 20 g; Chol 56 mg; Sod 384 mg.

Royal Raspberry Cake

Yield: 20 servings   Utensil: cake pan   Preheat: 350 degrees

2 cups flour
½ teaspoon salt
1 tablespoon baking powder
⅓ cup butter, softened
1 cup sugar
1 egg, beaten
1 cup milk
1 teaspoon vanilla extract
3½ cups fresh raspberries
1½ cups confectioners' sugar
2 tablespoons milk
2 tablespoons butter, melted
1 teaspoon vanilla extract

Combine flour, salt and baking powder in bowl; stir with whisk. Cream softened butter and sugar in large bowl until light and fluffy. Add egg; beat for 1 minute. Mix 1 cup milk and 1 teaspoon vanilla in small bowl. Add to creamed mixture alternately with dry ingredients, beating well after each addition. Pour into greased 9x13-inch cake pan. Spread raspberries evenly over batter. Bake at 350 degrees for 30 to 35 minutes or until cake tests done. Cool in pan for 5 minutes. Combine confectioners' sugar, 2 tablespoons milk, melted butter and 1 teaspoon vanilla in bowl; mix well. Spread over cake. Serve warm with vanilla ice cream. May substitute frozen raspberries for fresh raspberries.

Approx Per Serving: Cal 179; Prot 2 g; Carbo 32 g; Fiber 2 g; T Fat 5 g; Chol 24 mg; Sod 148 mg.

Rum Cake

Yield: 16 servings *Utensil: bundt pan* *Preheat: 350 degrees*

2 cups sugar
1 cup shortening
4 eggs
3 cups flour
1 teaspoon baking powder
½ teaspoon soda
1 cup buttermilk
1 teaspoon lemon extract
1 teaspoon rum extract
1 teaspoon vanilla extract
1 cup sugar
½ cup water
1 tablespoon rum extract

Cream 2 cups sugar and shortening in large bowl until light and fluffy. Add eggs 1 at a time, beating well after each addition. Sift flour, baking powder and soda together twice. Add to creamed mixture alternately with buttermilk, beating well after each addition. Stir in 1 teaspoon each of lemon, rum and vanilla extracts. Pour into greased and floured bundt pan. Bake at 350 degrees for 1 hour or until cake tests done. Cool in pan for 5 minutes. Combine 1 cup sugar with water in saucepan. Cook over medium heat until glaze begins to form, stirring constantly. Stir in 1 tablespoon rum extract. Remove from heat; let stand until cool. Pour over warm cake. Invert onto cake plate when cool.

Approx Per Serving: Cal 368; Prot 4 g; Carbo 56 g; Fiber 1 g; T Fat 15 g; Chol 54 mg; Sod 81 mg.

Nutty Rich Rum Cake

Yield: 12 servings *Utensil: bundt pan* *Preheat: 325 degrees*

½ cup chopped pecans
1 2-layer package butter pecan cake mix
4 eggs, beaten
½ cup vegetable oil
½ cup water
½ cup light rum
1 4-ounce package vanilla instant pudding mix
½ cup butter
1 cup sugar
¼ cup rum
¼ cup water

Place pecans in bottom of greased and floured bundt pan. Combine cake mix, eggs, oil, ½ cup water, ½ cup rum and pudding mix in large bowl; beat well. Pour into prepared pan. Bake at 325 degrees for 40 minutes. Combine ½ cup butter, sugar, ¼ cup rum and ¼ cup water in saucepan. Bring to a boil. Cook for 10 minutes, stirring constantly. Pour over warm cake. Leave cake in pan for 1 to 2 days. Turn onto serving plate before serving.

Approx Per Serving: Cal 512; Prot 4 g; Carbo 60 g; Fiber <1 g; T Fat 26 g; Chol 92 mg; Sod 397 mg.

Strawberry Shortcake

Yield: 15 servings   Utensil: cake pan   Preheat: 350 degrees

1 10-ounce package miniature marshmallows
1 2-layer package yellow cake mix
1 3-ounce package strawberry gelatin
1 16-ounce package frozen strawberries, thawed, sliced
½ cup cold water

Line greased 9x13-inch cake pan with marshmallows. Prepare cake mix using package directions. Pour over marshmallows. Sprinkle gelatin over batter. Spoon undrained strawberries over top. Drizzle with water. Bake at 350 degrees for 1 hour or until cake tests done. Marshmallows will rise to the top and strawberries will sink to the bottom. Cool on wire rack; turn onto serving plate.

Approx Per Serving: Cal 238; Prot 3 g; Carbo 52 g; Fiber 1 g; T Fat 3 g; Chol 0 mg; Sod 245 mg.

Weatherman's Cake

Yield: 15 servings   Utensil: cake pan   Preheat: 350 degrees

1 cup boiling water
1 cup dates, chopped
1 teaspoon soda
1 tablespoon baking cocoa
½ cup margarine, softened
1 cup sugar
2 teaspoons vanilla extract
2 eggs, beaten
1¾ cups flour
½ teaspoon salt
1 cup chocolate chips
½ cup chopped pecans

Pour boiling water over dates in small bowl. Let stand to cool. Stir in soda and cocoa; set aside. Cream margarine and sugar in large bowl until light and fluffy. Add vanilla and eggs, beating well. Stir in flour, salt and date mixture. Pour into greased 9x13-inch cake pan. Sprinkle chocolate chips and pecans over batter. Bake at 350 degrees for 30 to 35 minutes or until cake tests done. Cool on wire rack. May sprinkle cooled cake with confectioners' sugar.

Approx Per Serving: Cal 287; Prot 3 g; Carbo 41 g; Fiber 2 g; T Fat 14 g; Chol 28 mg; Sod 209 mg.

Marble-Top Apricot Pie

Yield: 8 servings Utensil: pie plate Preheat: no

1/2 cup sugar
1/3 cup flour
1/4 teaspoon salt
3/4 cup milk
1 1/4 cups puréed apricots
2 egg yolks, beaten
2 tablespoons butter or margarine
Juice of 1 lemon
1 9-inch baked pie shell
8 ounces whipped topping
1/4 square unsweetened chocolate

Place sugar, flour, salt and milk in double boiler. Cook over medium heat until thickened, stirring constantly. Remove from heat. Add apricots and egg yolks gradually, stirring constantly. Cook for 5 to 10 minutes longer, stirring frequently. Mix in butter and lemon juice. Cool. Pour into 9-inch pie shell. Spread with whipped cream. Place chocolate in small glass container. Microwave on High for 2 minutes or until melted. Cool. Pour over whipped cream, spreading to give marble appearance.

Approx Per Serving: Cal 359; Prot 4 g; Carbo 41 g; Fiber 1 g; T Fat 20 g; Chol 64 mg; Sod 249 mg.

Cherry Tarts

Yield: 8 servings Utensil: muffin pan Preheat: 375 degrees

1 8-count can crescent rolls
3 ounces cream cheese, softened
2 tablespoons sugar
1/4 cup sour cream
1/2 teaspoon almond extract
1 21-ounce can cherry pie filling
1/3 cup sliced almonds

Press crescent roll dough into each muffin cup to form shell. Beat cream cheese, sugar, sour cream and almond extract in bowl until smooth. Place a small amount of mixture in each muffin cup. Top with cherry pie filling. Sprinkle with sliced almonds. Bake at 375 degrees for 22 to 27 minutes.

Approx Per Serving: Cal 285; Prot 4 g; Carbo 35 g; Fiber 2 g; T Fat 15 g; Chol 15 mg; Sod 289 mg.

Bishop's Chocolate Pie

Yield: 6 servings   *Utensil: pie plate*   *Preheat: no*

1 2/3 cups graham cracker crumbs
1/4 cup butter, softened
1/4 cup sugar
1 4-ounce package vanilla instant pudding mix
1 4-ounce package chocolate instant pudding mix
2 cups milk
1 teaspoon vanilla extract
2 cups vanilla ice cream, softened
8 ounces whipped topping

Combine graham cracker crumbs, butter and sugar in small bowl; mix well. Press into 9-inch pie plate. Combine vanilla and chocolate puddings with milk in mixer bowl, stirring until dissolved. Add vanilla and ice cream. Beat just until blended. Pour into prepared pie shell. Chill in refrigerator. Spread with whipped topping. Garnish with chocolate curls. May also prepare Banana Pie by using 2 packages vanilla pudding mix and 2 bananas, sliced; omit chocolate curls.

Approx Per Serving: Cal 607; Prot 7 g; Carbo 84 g; Fiber 1 g; T Fat 28 g; Chol 51 mg; Sod 541 mg.

Coconut Angel Pie

Yield: 8 servings   *Utensil: deep-dish pie plate*   *Preheat: 275 degrees*

1 1/3 cups graham cracker crumbs
1/2 cup melted butter
4 egg whites
1/4 teaspoon salt
1 teaspoon vinegar
1 cup sugar
1 cup sliced peaches
8 ounces whipping cream, whipped
1/2 cup shredded coconut
2 tablespoons sugar
1 teaspoon vanilla extract

Mix graham cracker crumbs and butter together in bowl. Press into 9-inch deep dish pie plate. Beat egg whites at medium speed in mixer bowl until soft peaks form. Add salt and vinegar. Beat at high speed until stiff peaks form. Add 1 cup sugar 2 tablespoonfuls at a time, beating well after each addition. Spread into prepared pie shell. Bake at 275 degrees for 1 1/2 hours. Cool. Arrange peach slices over cooled meringue. Spread with whipped cream. Mix coconut, 2 tablespoons sugar and vanilla in ovenproof dish. Broil until golden brown; watch carefully. Cool. Sprinkle over whipped cream. Chill in refrigerator before serving.

Approx Per Serving: Cal 419; Prot 4 g; Carbo 45 g; Fiber 1 g; T Fat 26 g; Chol 72 mg; Sod 302 mg.

Custard Pie

Yield: 6 servings	Utensil: pie plate	Preheat: 350 degrees

1 tablespoon (scant) flour
3 tablespoons (heaping) sugar
1/8 teaspoon salt
3 eggs, well beaten
2 cups milk
1 unbaked 8-inch pie shell

Combine flour, sugar, salt, eggs and milk in bowl; mix well. Pour into unbaked 8-inch pie shell. Bake at 350 degrees for 40 minutes or until knife inserted near center comes out clean. May sprinkle with nutmeg.

Approx Per Serving: Cal 268; Prot 8 g; Carbo 26 g; Fiber <1 g; T Fat 16 g; Chol 117 mg; Sod 296 mg.

Key Lime Pie

Yield: 8 servings	Utensil: pie plate	Preheat: no

1 6-ounce can frozen limeade concentrate
1 14-ounce can sweetened condensed milk
8 ounces whipped topping
1 8-inch graham cracker pie shell

Thaw limeade concentrate. Combine with sweetened condensed milk in bowl; blend well. Fold in whipped topping. Spoon mixture into pie shell. Chill in refrigerator until firm.

Approx Per Serving: Cal 403; Prot 4 g; Carbo 54 g; Fiber 1 g; T Fat 20 g; Chol 7 mg; Sod 273 mg.

Soda Cracker Peach Pie

Yield: 8 servings	Utensil: pie plate	Preheat: 325 degrees

3 egg whites
1 cup sugar
1 teaspoon vanilla extract
12 soda crackers, crushed
1/4 teaspoon baking powder
1/2 cup pecans
8 peaches, peeled, sliced
1 cup whipped cream
Cinnamon to taste

Beat egg whites at medium speed in mixer bowl until soft peaks form. Add sugar and vanilla gradually, beating at high speed until stiff peaks form. Mix crushed crackers with baking powder and pecans. Fold into egg whites gently. Spoon into well greased 9-inch pie plate. Bake at 325 degrees for 30 minutes. Cool. Fill with sliced peaches. Top with whipped cream, sealing to edge. Sprinkle with cinnamon. Chill for 6 to 12 hours before serving.

Approx Per Serving: Cal 259; Prot 3 g; Carbo 40 g; Fiber 2 g; T Fat 11 g; Chol 22 mg; Sod 93 mg.

Equivalent Chart

	When the recipe calls for	Use
Baking	1/2 cup butter 2 cups butter 4 cups all-purpose flour 4 1/2 to 5 cups sifted cake flour 1 square chocolate 1 cup semisweet chocolate chips 4 cups marshmallows 2 1/4 cups packed brown sugar 4 cups confectioners' sugar 2 cups granulated sugar	4 ounces 1 pound 1 pound 1 pound 1 ounce 6 ounces 1 pound 1 pound 1 pound 1 pound
Cereal – Bread	1 cup fine dry bread crumbs 1 cup soft bread crumbs 1 cup small bread cubes 1 cup fine cracker crumbs 1 cup fine graham cracker crumbs 1 cup vanilla wafer crumbs 1 cup crushed cornflakes 4 cups cooked macaroni 3 1/2 cups cooked rice	4 to 5 slices 2 slices 2 slices 28 saltines 15 crackers 22 wafers 3 cups uncrushed 8 ounces uncooked 1 cup uncooked
Dairy	1 cup shredded cheese 1 cup cottage cheese 1 cup sour cream 1 cup whipped cream 2/3 cup evaporated milk 1 2/3 cups evaporated milk	4 ounces 8 ounces 8 ounces 1/2 cup heavy cream 1 small can 1 13-ounce can
Fruit	4 cups sliced or chopped apples 1 cup mashed bananas 2 cups pitted cherries 2 1/2 cups shredded coconut 4 cups cranberries 1 cup pitted dates 1 cup candied fruit 3 to 4 tablespoons lemon juice plus 1 tablespoon grated lemon rind 1/3 cup orange juice plus 2 teaspoons grated orange rind 4 cups sliced peaches 2 cups pitted prunes 3 cups raisins	4 medium 3 medium 4 cups unpitted 8 ounces 1 pound 1 8-ounce package 1 8-ounce package 1 lemon 1 orange 8 medium 1 12-ounce package 1 15-ounce package

	When the recipe calls for	Use
Meats	4 cups chopped cooked chicken 3 cups chopped cooked meat 2 cups cooked ground meat	1 5-pound chicken 1 pound, cooked 1 pound, cooked
Nuts	1 cup chopped nuts	4 ounces shelled 1 pound unshelled
Vegetables	2 cups cooked green beans 2½ cups lima beans or red beans 4 cups shredded cabbage 1 cup grated carrot 8 ounces fresh mushrooms 1 cup chopped onion 4 cups sliced or chopped potatoes 2 cups canned tomatoes	½ pound fresh or 1 16-ounce can 1 cup dried, cooked 1 pound 1 large 1 4-ounce can 1 large 4 medium 1 16-ounce can

Measurement Equivalents

1 tablespoon = 3 teaspoons
2 tablespoons = 1 ounce
4 tablespoons = ¼ cup
5⅓ tablespoons = ⅓ cup
8 tablespoons = ½ cup
12 tablespoons = ¾ cup
16 tablespoons = 1 cup
1 cup = 8 ounces or ½ pint
4 cups = 1 quart
4 quarts = 1 gallon

1 6½ to 8-ounce can = 1 cup
1 10½ to 12-ounce can = 1¼ cups
1 14 to 16-ounce can = 1¾ cups
1 16 to 17-ounce can = 2 cups
1 18 to 20-ounce can = 2½ cups
1 29-ounce can = 3½ cups
1 46 to 51-ounce can = 5¾ cups
1 6½ to 7½-pound can or
   Number 10 = 12 to 13 cups

Metric Equivalents

Liquid

1 teaspoon = 5 milliliters
1 tablespoon = 15 milliliters
1 fluid ounce = 30 milliliters
1 cup = 250 milliliters
1 pint = 500 milliliters

Dry

1 quart = 1 liter
1 ounce = 30 grams
1 pound = 450 grams
2.2 pounds = 1 kilogram

NOTE: *The metric measures are approximate benchmarks for purposes of home food preparation.*

Substitution Chart

	Instead of	Use
Baking	1 teaspoon baking powder	¼ teaspoon soda plus ½ teaspoon cream of tartar
	1 tablespoon cornstarch (for thickening)	2 tablespoons flour or 1 tablespoon tapioca
	1 cup sifted all-purpose flour	1 cup plus 2 tablespoons sifted cake flour
	1 cup sifted cake flour	1 cup minus 2 tablespoons sifted all-purpose flour
	1 cup dry bread crumbs	¾ cup cracker crumbs
Dairy	1 cup buttermilk	1 cup sour milk or 1 cup yogurt
	1 cup heavy cream	¾ cup skim milk plus ⅓ cup butter
	1 cup light cream	⅞ cup skim milk plus 3 tablespoons butter
	1 cup sour cream	⅞ cup sour milk plus 3 tablespoons butter
	1 cup sour milk	1 cup milk plus 1 tablespoon vinegar or lemon juice or 1 cup buttermilk
Seasoning	1 teaspoon allspice	½ teaspoon cinnamon plus ⅛ teaspoon cloves
	1 cup catsup	1 cup tomato sauce plus ½ cup sugar plus 2 tablespoons vinegar
	1 clove of garlic	⅛ teaspoon garlic powder or ⅛ teaspoon instant minced garlic or ¾ teaspoon garlic salt or 5 drops of liquid garlic
	1 teaspoon Italian spice	¼ teaspoon each oregano, basil, thyme, rosemary plus dash of cayenne
	1 teaspoon lemon juice	½ teaspoon vinegar
	1 tablespoon mustard	1 teaspoon dry mustard
	1 medium onion	1 tablespoon dried minced onion or 1 teaspoon onion powder
Sweet	1 1-ounce square chocolate	¼ cup cocoa plus 1 teaspoon shortening
	1⅔ ounces semisweet chocolate	1 ounce unsweetened chocolate plus 4 teaspoons granulated sugar
	1 cup honey	1 to 1¼ cups sugar plus ¼ cup liquid or 1 cup corn syrup or molasses
	1 cup granulated sugar	1 cup packed brown sugar or 1 cup corn syrup, molasses or honey minus ¼ cup liquid

CALORIE CHART

Almonds, shelled, 1/4 cup	213
Apples: 1 med	70
chopped, 1/2 cup	30
juice, 1 cup	117
Applesauce, 1/2 cup: sweetened	115
unsweetened	50
Apricots: canned, 1/2 cup	110
dried, 10 halves	100
fresh, 3	55
nectar, 1 cup	140
Asparagus: canned, 1/2 cup	18
fresh, 6 spears	19
Avocado, 1 med	265
Bacon, crisp-cooked, 2 slices	90
Banana, 1 med	100
Beans, 1/2 cup: baked	160
dried	350
green	20
lima	95
soy	95
Bean sprouts, 1/2 cup	18
Beef, cooked, 3 oz:	
broiled, sirloin steak	330
roasted, heel of round	165
roasted, rib	375
Beer, 12 oz	150
Beets, cooked, 1/2 cup	40
Biscuit, from mix, 1	90
Bologna, all meat, 3 oz	235
Bread: 1 roll	85
white, 1 slice	65
whole wheat, 1 slice	55
Bread crumbs, dry, 1 cup	390
Broccoli, cooked, 1/2 cup	20
Butter, 1 tbsp	100
Buttermilk, 1 cup	90
Cabbage, 1/2 cup: cooked	15
fresh, shredded	10
Cake, 1/12 cake: angel food	140
devil's food	195
yellow	200
Candy, 1 oz: caramel	115
chocolate, sweet	145
hard candy	110
marshmallows	90
Cantaloupe, 1/2 med	60
Carrots: cooked, 1/2 cup	23
fresh, 1 med	20
Catsup, 1 tbsp	18
Cauliflower: cooked, 1/2 cup	13
fresh, 1/2 lb	60
Celery, chopped, 1/2 cup	8
Cereals, 1/2 cup: bran flakes	53
cornflakes	50
oatmeal, cooked	65
Cheese: American, 1 oz	105
Cheddar, 1 oz	113
cottage: creamed, 1/2 cup	130
uncreamed, 1/2 cup	85
cream, 1 oz	107
mozzarella, 1 oz	80
Parmesan, 1 oz	110
Velveeta, 1 oz	84
Cherries, 1/2 cup: canned, sour	53
fresh, sweet	40
Chicken, cooked, 4 oz:	
broiled	155
canned, boned	230
roasted, dark meat	210
roasted, light meat	207
Chilies, fresh, 8 oz: green	62
red	108
Chili powder, 1 tbsp	51
Chocolate, baking, 1 oz	143
Cocoa mix, 1 oz	115
Cocoa, unsweetened, 1/3 cup	120
Coconut, shredded, 1/4 cup	166
Coffee	0
Corn, 1/2 cup: cream-style	100
whole kernel	85
Corn bread, 1x4-in. piece	125
Corn chips, 1 oz	130
Cornmeal, 1/2 cup	264
Cornstarch, 1 tbsp	29
Crab meat, 3 oz: canned	85
fresh	80
Crackers: graham, 1 square	28
Ritz, 1	17
saltine, 1 square	13
Cracker crumbs, 1/2 cup	281
Cranberries: fresh, 1/2 lb	100
juice, cocktail, 1 cup	163
sauce, 1/2 cup	190
Cream, 1 tbsp: half and half	20
heavy	55
light	30
Creamer, nondairy, 1 tsp	10
Cucumber, 1 med	30
Dates, chopped, 1/2 cup	244
Eggs: 1 whole, large	80

Item	Calories
1 white	17
1 yolk	59
Eggplant, cooked, 1/2 cup	19
Fish sticks, 5	200
Flour, 1 cup: all-purpose	420
rye	286
whole wheat	400
Fruit cocktail, canned, 1/2 cup	98
Garlic, 1 clove	2
Gelatin, unflavored, 1 env.	25
Grapes: fresh, 1/2 cup	35-50
juice, 1 cup	170
Grapefruit: fresh, 1/2 med	60
juice, unsweetened, 1 cup	100
Ground beef, cooked, 3 oz:	
lean	185
regular	245
Haddock, fried, 3 oz	140
Ham, cooked, 3 oz:	
boiled	200
country-style	335
cured, lean	160
roasted, fresh	320
Honey, 1 tbsp.	65
Ice cream, 1/2 cup	135
Ice milk, 1/2 cup	96
Jams and preserves, 1 tbsp	54
Jellies, 1 tbsp	55
Jell-O, 1/2 cup	80
Lamb, cooked, 3 oz:	
broiled, rib chop	175
roasted, leg	185
Lemonade, sweetened, 1 cup	110
Lemon juice, 1 tbsp	4
Lentils, cooked, 1/2 cup	168
Lettuce, 1 head	40
Liver, 2 oz: beef, fried	130
chicken, simmered	88
Lobster, 2 oz	55
Macaroni, cooked, 1/2 cup	90
Mango, 1 fresh	134
Margarine, 1 tbsp	100
Mayonnaise, 1 tbsp	100
Milk, 1 cup: condensed	982
evaporated	385
nonfat dry	251
skim	89
2%	145
whole	160
Mushrooms: canned, 1/2 cup	20
fresh, 1 lb.	123
Mustard, prepared, 1 tbsp:	
brown	13
yellow	10
Nectarine, 1 fresh	30
Noodles: egg, cooked, 1/2 cup	100
fried, chow mein, 2 oz	275
Oil, cooking, salad, 1 tbsp	120
Okra, cooked, 8 pods	25
Olives: green, 3 lg	15
ripe, 2 lg	15
Onion: chopped, 1/2 cup	32
green, 6	20
Oranges: 1 med	65
juice, 1 cup	115
Oysters, 1/2 cup	80
Peaches: canned, 1/2 cup	100
dried, 1/2 cup	210
1 med	35
Peanuts, roasted, 1 cup	420
Peanut butter, 1 tbsp	100
Pears: canned, 1/2 cup	97
dried, 1/2 cup	214
fresh, 1 med	100
Peas, 1/2 cup: black-eyed	70
green, canned	83
green, frozen	69
Pecans, chopped, 1/2 cup	400
Peppers, sweet. 1 med: green	14
red	19
Perch, white, 4 oz	50
Pickles: dill, 1 lg	15
sweet, 1 med	30
Pie, 1/6 pie:	
apple	420
cherry	402
custard	330
pumpkin	321
Pie crust, mix, 1 crust	626
Pimento, canned, 1 med	10
Pineapple: canned, 1/2 cup	90
fresh, 1/2 cup	36
juice, 1 cup	135
Plums: canned, 3	101
fresh, 1 med	30
Popcorn, popped, 1 cup: plain	23
with oil and salt	40
Pork, cooked, lean:	
broiled, chop, 3.5 oz	260
roasted, Boston Butt, 4 oz	280
roasted, loin, 4 oz	290
Potato chips, 10 med	114
Potatoes, white:	
baked, with skin, 1 sm	93
boiled, 1 sm	70
French-fried, 10 pieces	175
hashed brown, 1/2 cup	177
mashed, 1/2 cup	90

Potatoes, sweet:			cream of chicken	235
baked, 1 med		155	cream of mushroom	331
candied, 1 med		295	tomato	220
canned, 1/2 cup		110	vegetable-beef	198
Prunes: dried, cooked, 1/2 cup		137	Sour cream, 1/2 cup	240
fresh, 1 lg		19	Spaghetti, cooked, 1/2 cup	80
juice, 1 cup		197	Spinach: cooked, 1/2 cup	20
Puddings, instant, prepared, 1/2 cup:			fresh, 1/2 lb	60
			Squash: summer, 1/2 cup	15
banana		175	winter, 1/2 cup	65
butterscotch		175	Strawberries, fresh, 1/2 cup	23
chocolate		200	Sugar: brown, 1/2 cup	410
lemon		180	confectioners', 1/2 cup	240
Puddings, pie fillings, prepared, 1/2 cup:			granulated, 1/2 cup	385
			1 tbsp.	48
banana		165	Syrups, 1 tbsp: chocolate	50
butterscotch		190	corn	58
chocolate		190	maple	50
lemon		125	Taco shell, 1 shell	50
Pumpkin, canned, 1/2 cup		38	Tomatoes: canned, 1/2 cup	25
Raisins, 1/2 cup		231	fresh, 1 med	40
Rice, cooked, 1/2 cup:			juice, 1 cup	45
brown		100	paste, 6-oz	150
minute		105	sauce, 8-oz	34
white		90	Toppings, 1 tbsp: caramel	70
Salad dressings, 1 tbsp:			chocolate fudge	65
blue cheese		75	Cool Whip	14
French		70	Dream Whip	8
Italian		83	strawberry	60
mayonnaise		100	Tortilla, corn, 1	65
mayonnaise-type		65	Tuna, canned, 4 oz:	
Russian		75	in oil	230
Thousand Island		80	in water	144
Salami, cooked, 2 oz		180	Turkey, roasted, 4 oz:	
Salmon, 4 oz: canned		180	dark meat	230
steak		220	light meat	200
Sardines, canned, 3 oz		75	Veal, cooked, 3 oz:	
Sauces, 1 tbsp: barbecue		17	broiled, cutlet	185
hot pepper		3	roasted	230
soy		9	Vegetable juice cocktail, 1 cup	43
tartar		74	Vinegar, 1 tbsp	2
white, med		215	Waffles, 1	130
Worcestershire		15	Walnuts, chopped, 1/2 cup	410
Sauerkraut, 1/2 cup		21	Water chestnuts, 1/2 cup	25
Sausage, cooked, 2 oz		260	Watermelon, fresh, 1/2 cup	26
Sherbet, 1/2 cup		130	Wheat germ, 1 tbsp	29
Shrimp: canned, 4 oz		130	Yeast: cake, 1 oz	24
cooked, 3 oz		50	dry, 1 oz	80
Soft drinks, 1 cup		100	Yogurt, 1 cup: plain	153
Soup, condensed, 1 can:			plain, skim milk	123
chicken with rice		116	plain whole milk	139
cream of celery		215	with fruit	260

Herbs

Use fresh whole herbs when possible. When fresh herbs are not available, use whole dried herbs that can be crushed just while adding. Store herbs in airtight containers away from the heat of the stove. Fresh herbs may be layered between paper towels and dried in the microwave on HIGH for 2 minutes or until dry.

Basil	Can be chopped and added to cold poultry salads. If the recipe calls for tomatoes or tomato sauce, add a touch of basil to bring out a rich flavor.
Bay leaf	The basis of many French seasonings. It is added to soups, stews, marinades and stuffings.
Bouquet garni	A bundle of parsley, thyme and bay leaves tied together and added to stews, soups or sauces. Other herbs and spices may be added to the basic herbs.
Chervil	One of the traditional *fines herbes* used in French cooking. (The others are tarragon, parsley and chives.) It is good in omelets and soups.
Chives	Available fresh, dried or frozen, it can be substituted for raw onion or shallot in nearly any recipe.
Garlic	One of the oldest herbs in the world, it must be carefully handled. For best results, press or crush the garlic clove.
Marjoram	An aromatic herb of the mint family, it is good in soups, sauces, stuffings and stews.
Mint	Use fresh, dried or ground with vegetables, desserts, fruits, jelly, lamb or tea. Fresh sprigs of mint make attractive aromatic garnishes.
Oregano	A staple, savory herb in Italian, Spanish, Greek and Mexican cuisines. It is very good in dishes with a tomato foundation, especially in combination with basil.
Parsley	Use this mild herb as fresh sprigs or dried flakes to flavor or garnish almost any dish.
Rosemary	This pungent herb is especially good in poultry and fish dishes and in such accompaniments as stuffings.
Saffron	Use this deep orange herb, made from the dried stamens of a crocus, sparingly in poultry, seafood and rice dishes.
Sage	This herb is a perennial favorite with all kinds of poultry and stuffings.
Tarragon	One of the *fines herbes*. Goes well with all poultry dishes whether hot or cold.
Thyme	Usually used in combination with bay leaf in soups, stews and sauces.

SPICES

Spices should be stored in airtight containers away from the heat of the stove or in the refrigerator. Add ground spices toward the end of the cooking time to retain maximum flavor. Whole spices may be added at the beginning but should have a small amount of additional spices added near the end of cooking time also.

Allspice	Pungent aromatic spice, whole or in powdered form. It is excellent in marinades, particularly in game marinade, or in curries.
Caraway seed	Use the whole seeds in breads, especially rye, and with cheese, sauerkraut and cabbage dishes.
Celery seed	Use whole or ground in salad dressings, sauces, pickles or meat, cheese, egg and fish dishes.
Chili powder	Made from dried red chili peppers, this spice ranges from mild to fiery depending on the type of chili pepper used. Used especially in Mexican cooking, it is a delicious addition to eggs, dips and sauces.
Cinnamon	Ground from the bark of the cinnamon tree, it is delicious in desserts as well as savory dishes.
Coriander	Seed used whole or ground, this slightly lemony spice adds an unusual flavor to soups, stews, chili dishes, curries and desserts.
Curry powder	A blend of several spices, this gives Indian cooking its characteristic flavor.
Cumin	A staple spice in Mexican cooking. Use in meat, rice, cheese, egg and fish dishes.
Ginger	The whole root used fresh, dried or ground is a sweet, pungent addition to desserts or oriental-style dishes.
Mustard (dry)	Ground mustard seed brings a sharp bite to sauces or may be sprinkled sparingly over poultry or other foods.
Nutmeg	Use the whole spice or a bit of freshly ground for flavor in beverages, breads and desserts. A sprinkle on top is both a flavor enhancer and an attractive garnish.
Pepper	Black and white pepper from the pepperberry or peppercorn, whether whole, ground or cracked, is the most commonly used spice in or on any food.
Poppy seed	Use these tiny, nutty-flavored seeds in salad dressings, breads, cakes or as a flavorful garnish for cheese, rolls or noodle dishes.
Turmeric	Ground from a root related to ginger, this is an essential in curry powder. Also used in pickles, relishes, cheese and egg dishes.

Quantities to Serve 100

Baked beans	5 gallons
Beef	40 pounds
Beets	30 pounds
Bread	10 loaves
Butter	3 pounds
Cabbage for slaw	20 pounds
Cakes	8 cakes
Carrots	33 pounds
Cauliflower	18 pounds
Cheese	18 pounds
Chicken for chicken pie	40 pounds
Coffee	3 pounds
Cream	3 quarts
Fruit cocktail	1 gallon
Fruit juice	4 (No. 10) cans
Fruit salad	20 quarts
Ground beef	30 to 36 pounds
Ham	40 pounds
Ice cream	4 gallons
Lettuce	20 heads
Meat loaf	24 pounds
Milk	6 gallons
Nuts	3 pounds
Olives	1 3/4 pounds
Oysters	18 quarts
Pickles	2 quarts
Pies	17 pies
Potatoes	35 pounds
Roast pork	40 pounds
Rolls	200 rolls
Salad dressing	3 quarts
Scalloped potatoes	5 gallons
Soup	5 gallons
Sugar cubes	3 pounds
Tomato juice	4 (No. 10) cans
Vegetables	4 (No. 20) cans
Vegetable salad	20 quarts
Whipping cream	4 pints
Wieners	25 pounds

NUTRITIONAL GUIDELINES

The editors have attempted to present these family recipes in a form that allows approximate nutritional values to be computed. Persons with dietary or health problems or whose diets require close monitoring should not rely solely on the nutritional information provided. They should consult their physicians or a registered dietitian for specific information.

Abbreviations for Nutritional Analysis

Cal — Calories
Prot — Protein
Carbo — Carbohydrates
Dietary Fiber — Fiber
T Fat — Total Fat
Chol — Cholesterol
Sod — Sodium
gr — gram
mg — milligrams

Nutritional information for these recipes is computed from information derived from many sources, including materials supplied by the United States Department of Agriculture, computer databanks and journals in which the information is assumed to be in the public domain. However, many specialty items, new products and processed foods may not be available from these sources or may vary from the average values used in these analyses. More information on new and/or specific products may be obtained by reading the nutrient labels. Unless otherwise specified, the nutritional analysis of these recipes is based on all measurements being level.

- **Artificial sweeteners** vary in use and strength so should be used "to taste," using the recipe ingredients as a guideline.
- **Artificial sweeteners** using aspartame (NutraSweet and Equal) should not be used as a sweetener in recipes involving prolonged heating which reduces the sweet taste. For further information on the use of these sweeteners, refer to package information.
- **Alcoholic ingredients** have been analyzed for the basic ingredients, although cooking causes the evaporation of alcohol thus decreasing caloric content.
- **Buttermilk, sour cream** and **yogurt** are the types available commercially.
- **Cake mixes** which are prepared using package directions include 3 eggs and 1/2 cup oil.
- **Chicken**, cooked for boning and chopping, has been roasted; this method yields the lowest caloric values.
- **Cottage cheese** is cream-style with 4.2% creaming mixture. Dry-curd cottage cheese has no creaming mixture.
- **Eggs** are all large.
- **Flour** is unsifted all-purpose flour.
- **Garnishes**, serving suggestions and other optional additions and variations are not included in the analysis.
- **Margarine** and **butter** are regular, not whipped or presoftened.
- **Milk** is whole milk, 3.5% butterfat. Lowfat milk is 1% butterfat. Evaporated milk is whole milk with 60% of the water removed.
- **Oil** is any type of vegetable cooking oil. Shortening is hydrogenated vegetable shortening.
- **Salt** and other ingredients to taste as noted in the ingredients have not been included in the nutritional analysis.
- If a choice of ingredients has been given, the nutritional analysis reflects the first option.

INDEX

APPETIZERS
  Cheese Chili Squares, 20
  Crabmeat Canapés, 20
  Dip for Strawberries, 23
  Fluffy Fruit Dip, 23
  Hot Crabmeat Spread, 24
  Liver Pâté, 25
  New Potato Appetizers, 22
  Pary Spread, 24
  Sausage Puffs, 22
  Spinach-Stuffed Mushrooms, 21
  Stuffed Mushrooms, 21
  Taco Dip, 23

BEEF. *See also* Ground Beef; Veal
  Corned Beef Salad, 45
  Easy Pepper Steak, 57
  Gourmet Beef and Lobster, 56
  Marinated Shish Kabob, 58
  Onion-Buttered Sirloin, 57
  Pepper Steak, 56
  Reuben Casserole, 59
  Slow-Cooking Stew, 59
  Sunday Roast, 58

BEVERAGES
  Holiday Punch, 25
  Hot 'n' Spicy Punch, 26
  Orange Julius, 26
  Wedding Punch, 26

BREADS
  Cinnamon Delight, 104
  Expand Your Bread-Baking Repertory, 114
  Mom's Pizza Crust, 111

BREADS, LOAVES
  Beer Bread, 105
  Delicious Cheese Bread, 113
  Dilly Bread, 106
  Dutch Apple Bread, 104
  Honey Whole Wheat Bread, 108
  Mustard Bread, 114
  Orange Pecan Bread, 106
  Pineapple Bread, 107
  Prize Banana Nut Bread, 105
  Pumpkin Date Bread, 107
  Strawberry Bread, 108

BREADS, MUFFINS
  Banana Oatbran Muffins, 109
  Bran Muffins, 109
  Pumpkin Apple Streusel Muffins, 110
  Sassy Cinnamon Muffins, 110
  Yogurt Date Muffins, 111

BREADS, ROLLS
  Hot Cross Buns, 112
  Pull-Apart Rolls, 112
  Sweet Dough, 113

BREADS, YEAST
  Dill Bread, 106
  Honey Whole Wheat Bread, 108
  Hot Cross Buns, 112
  Mom's Pizza Crust, 111
  Pull-Apart Rolls, 112
  Sweet Dough, 113

CAKES
  Apricot Brandy Cake, 137
  Aunt Ellen's Oatmeal Cake, 141
  Carrrot Cake, 137
  Delicate Cake, 139
  Depression Cake, 140
  Easy Carrot Cake, 138
  Fresh Apple Cake with Hot Sauce, 136
  Heath Bar Cake, 140
  Jewish Apple Cake, 136
  Lemon Cake, 141
  Low-Cholesterol Chocolate Cake, 138
  Nutty Rich Rum Cake, 143
  Pineapple Cake with Icing, 142
  Royal Raspberry Cake, 142
  Rum Cake, 143
  Strawberry Shortcake, 144
  Wacky Chocolate Delight, 139
  Weatherman's Cake, 144

CANDY
  Almond Bark Candy, 126

Bob's Favorite Candy, 127
Candied Lemon Peel, 127
Cheese Fudge, 126
Easy Peanut Brittle, 127
IMMC Peanut Butter
    Candy, 128
Never Fail Divinity, 126
Toffee Clusters, 128

CHICKEN. *See also* Turkey
Cheesy Chicken Corn
    Chowder, 31
Chicken à La King, 86
Chicken Cordon Bleu, 81
Chicken Creole, 82
Chicken Cutlets, 82
Chicken Parmigiana, 84
Chicken with Orange
    Sauce, 83
Chinese Stir-Fry, 85
Elegant Chicken, 77
Fruited Chicken Salad, 45
Ham and Chicken Casserole, 66
Hot Chicken Sandwiches, 36
IMMC Chicken Salad with
    Fruit, 46
Lemony Chicken, 83
Perfect Roasted Chicken, 76
Sauerkraut Soup, 35
Sautéed Chicken Breasts in
    Cream Sauce, 84
Stir-Fried Chicken and
    Vegetables, 85

CHICKEN, CASSEROLES
Chicken and Rice
    Casserole, 79
Chicken and Spaghetti
    Casserole, 80
Chicken Broccoli Casserole, 76
Chicken Divine, 77
Chicken Enchilada Bake, 78
Chicken in Wine and Cream
    Sauce, 87
Chicken Tetrazzini, 86
Chicken-Macaroni
    Casserole, 79
Hot Chicken Salad, 80
Huntington Chicken and
    Noodles, 81
Scalloped Chicken, 78

COOKIES
Apple Pie Bars, 129
Best Brownies, 129
Candied Fruit Brownies, 130
Chinese Almond Cookies, 128
Coconut-Walnut Shortbread
    Bars, 132
Famous Chocolate Chip
    Cookies, 132
IMMC Brownies with
    Walnuts, 130
IMMC Chocolate Chip
    Cookies, 131
IMMC Glazed Lemon Bars, 133
Oatmeal Caramel Bars, 133
Prize-Winning Hunka
    Chocolate Cookies, 131
Pumpkin Bars, 134
Whole Wheat Molasses Sugar
    Cookies, 134

DESSERTS. *See also* Cakes;
    Candy; Cookies; Pies
Almond Cream Sauce for
    Angel Food Cake, 116
Apple Dumplings, 116
Bailey's Irish Cream
    Cheesecake, 118
Buster Bar Dessert, 117
Caramel Bar, 118
Chocolate Almond
    Cheesecake, 119
Danish Puff, 119
IMMC Creamy Rice
    Pudding, 124
Praline Crêpes, 123

DESSERTS, FRUIT
Apple Bavarian Torte, 117
Fluffy Lemon Dessert, 120
Frozen Lemon Soufflé with
    Berry Sauce, 121
Frozen Lemon-Meringue
    Dessert, 120
Frozen Piña Colada Ice Cream
    Cake, 122
IMMC Tropical Rice
    Pudding, 124
Pear Clafouti, 122
Refrigerator Strawberry
    Dessert, 125

Steamed Cranberry Pudding, 123
Yummy Dessert, 125

EGG DISHES
Asparagus, Quiche, 72
Breakfast Bake, 70
Chile Cheese Squares, 20
Easy Blintz Bunch, 73
Egg-Asparagus Burritos, 73
Fancy Egg Scramble, 71

FROSTINGS
Pumpkin Bar Frosting, 134

GROUND BEEF
Barbecued Meatballs, 62
Beefy Baked Beans, 92
Beefy Spinach and Cheese Cassata, 60
Best-Ever Soup, 30
Enchilada Pie, 61
Ground Beef Upside-Down Corn Bread, 62
Meat Loaf, 63
Mexican Casserole, 61
Oven Porcupines, 63
Pizza Burger, 37
Spaghetti with Meat Sauce, 64
Stromboli Sandwich, 37
Taco Dip, 23
Taco Sandwiches, 38

HAM
Burgundy Ham with Green Grapes, 65
Garbanzo Soup, 32
Ham and Chicken Casserole, 66
Ham and Wild Rice Casserole, 67
Ham Hock Heaven, 33
Ham Rolls, 67
New Orleans Red Beans and Rice, 65
Swedish Ham Balls, 66

IMMC RECIPES
Brownies with Walnuts, 130
Chicken Salad with Fruit, 46
Chocolate Chip Cookies, 131
Creamy Rice Pudding, 124

Glazed Lemon Bars, 133
Homemade Italian Salad Dressing, 53
Peanut Butter Candy, 128
Spinach Leaf Salad, 53
Tropical Rice Pudding, 124

MEATBALLS
Barbecued Meatballs, 62
Ham Rolls, 67
Oven Porcupines, 63
Swedish Ham Balls, 66
Veal Meatballs, 64

MEATLESS MAIN DISHES
Asparagus Quiche, 72
Easy Blintz Brunch, 73
Egg-Asparagus Burritos, 73
Meatless Lasagna, 74
Quesadillas, 74

MICROWAVE
Chicken Enchilada Bake, 78
Pork Loin with Special Sauce, 68
Toffee Clusters, 128

MUFFINS. *See* Breads

PASTA
Chicken and Spaghetti Casserole, 80
Chicken Tetrazzini, 86
Fettucini, 71
Lasagna, 72
Meatless Lasagna, 74
Summer Pasta Salad, 46

PIES
Bishop's Chocolate Pie, 146
Cherry Tarts, 145
Coconut Angel Pie, 146
Custard Pie, 147
Key Lime Pie, 147
Marble-Top Apricot Pie, 145
Soda Cracker Peach Pie, 147

PORK. *See also* Ham; Sausage
Bacon-Wrapped Pork Loaves, 70
Baked Iowa Chops, 69

Fancy Egg Scramble, 71
Fettucini, 71
Ham Rolls, 67
Italian Chef's Prime, 68
Italian Sausage Soup, 33
Marinated Iowa Chops, 69
Pork Chops and Rice, 69
Pork Loin with Special
    Sauce, 68
Swedish Ham Balls, 66

PUNCHES. *See* Beverages

RICE
Chinese Fried Rice, 101
New Orleans Red Beans and
    Rice, 65
Simple Rice, 102
Wild Rice Pilaf, 101
Wild Rice Salad, 47
Wild Rice Soup, 35

ROLLS. *See* Breads

SALADS, DRESSINGS
Easy Bleu Cheese Dressing, 54
Honey Salad Dressing, 54
IMMC Homemade Italian Salad
    Dressing, 53
Salad Dressing for
    Coleslaw, 54

SALADS, FRUIT
Apricot Salad with Topping, 40
Cranberry-Cherry Salad, 40
Double Lemon Salad, 42
Fruit Basket Upset, 41
Fruity Cheese Salad, 41
Golden Fleck Salad, 42
Lime-Cheese Salad, 43
Peach Ambrosia Salad, 43
Quick Sunny Salad, 44
Raspberry Salad, 44

SALADS, MAIN DISH
Corned Beef Salad, 45
Fruited Chicken Salad, 45
IMMC Chicken Salad with
    Fruit, 46
Summer Pasta Salad, 46
Wild Rice Salad, 47

SALADS, VEGETABLE
Bacon and Cauliflower
    Salad, 48
Caesar Vegetable Salad, 47
Colonel Sander's Coleslaw, 49
Fresh Cauliflower and Broccoli
    Salad, 48
Go-With-Everything Salad, 50
IMMC Spinach Leaf Salad, 53
Lauri's Tossed Salad, 51
Layered Lettuce Salad, 50
Mom's Best Potato Salad, 51
Oriental Coleslaw, 49
Spinach Salad with Mustard-
    Bacon Dressing, 52
Strawberry-Spinach Salad, 52

SANDWICHES
Hot Chicken Sandwiches, 36
Pizza Burger, 37
Stromboli Sandwich, 37
Taco Sandwiches, 38
Tasty Tuna Crescents, 38

SAUCES
Almond Cream Sauce for
    Angel Food Cake, 116
Mustard Sauce, 102
Rarebit Topping, 102

SAUSAGE
Breakfast Bake, 70
Italian Sausage Soup, 33
Lasagna, 72
Sausage Puffs, 22

SEAFOOD
Artichoke Shrimp Soup, 29
Baked Shrimp Creole, 90
Chinese Fried Rice, 101
Crabmeat Canapés, 20
Fiery Cajun Shrimp, 89
Fish with Mustard Sauce, 88
Gourmet Beef and
    Lobster, 56
Hot Crabmeat Spread, 24
Sole Florentine, 88
Spicy Shrimp with
    Walnuts, 90
Tasty Tuna Crescents, 38
Yogurt Baked Fish, 89

SIDE DISHES. *See* Pasta; Rice; Sauces

SIDE DISHES, FRUIT
Cranberry Relish, 100
Scalloped Pineapple, 101

SOUPS
Artichoke Shrimp Soup, 29
Best-Ever Soup, 30
Borsch, 28
Cheese Soup, 31
Cheesy Chicken Corn Chowder, 31
Cucumber-Yogurt Soup, 28
Eggdrop Soup, 32
Garbanzo Soup, 32
Gazpacho, 29
Gourmet Vegetable Soup, 36
Ham Hock Heaven, 33
Italian Sausage Soup, 33
Potato Soup with Cheese and Bacon, 34
Potato Soup with Noodles, 34
Sauerkraut Soup, 35
Sour Cream-Broccoli Soup, 30
Wild Rice Soup, 35

TURKEY. *See also* Chicken
Marinated Turkey, 87
Sauerkraut Soup, 35

VEAL
Veal Meatballs, 64

VEGETABLES. *See* Salads
Beefy Baked Beans, 92
Candied Sweet Potatoes, 98
Golden Baked Onions, 94
Pea Casserole, 95
Sauerkraut Casserole, 97
Spinach Soufflé, 97
Swiss Vegetable Combo, 100
Tomato Pie, 98

VEGETABLES, ASPARAGUS
Asparagus Quiche, 72
Egg-Asparagus Burritos, 73

VEGETABLES, BROCCOLI
Sour Cream-Broccoli Soup, 30

VEGETABLES, CARROTS
Au Gratin Carrots, 92
Carrot and Rice Ring, 93

VEGETABLES, CORN
Corn Pudding, 94
Elegant Scalloped Corn, 93

VEGETABLES, MUSHROOMS
Spinach-Stuffed Mushrooms, 21
Stuffed Mushrooms, 21

VEGETABLES, POTATOES
Cheese Potatoes, 95
Creamy Potato Bake, 96
Italian Potatoes, 96
New Potato Appetizers, 22
Potato Soup with Cheese and Bacon, 34
Potato Soup with Noodles, 34

VEGETABLES, ZUCCHINI
Zucchini Casserole, 99
Zucchini-Pepper Sauté, 99

ORDER FORM: IOWA METHODIST BANQUET COOKBOOK
C/O IOWA METHODIST HEALTH FOUNDATION
1440 INGERSOLL, DES MOINES, IOWA 50309

Make checks payable to:
IOWA METHODIST HEALTH FOUNDATION

NAME _____

ADDRESS _____

CITY/STATE/ZIP _____

PLEASE SEND _____ COPIES   @ $10.00 EACH _____

POSTAGE & HANDLING   @ $ 2.00 EACH _____

                            TOTAL $ _____

COOKBOOKS MAY BE PURCHASED DIRECTLY
AT IOWA METHODIST HEALTH FOUNDATION

- -

ORDER FORM: IOWA METHODIST BANQUET COOKBOOK
C/O IOWA METHODIST HEALTH FOUNDATION
1440 INGERSOLL, DES MOINES, IOWA 50309

Make checks payable to:
IOWA METHODIST HEALTH FOUNDATION

NAME _____

ADDRESS _____

CITY/STATE/ZIP _____

PLEASE SEND _____ COPIES   @ $10.00 EACH _____

POSTAGE & HANDLING   @ $ 2.00 EACH _____

                            TOTAL $ _____

COOKBOOKS MAY BE PURCHASED DIRECTLY
AT IOWA METHODIST HEALTH FOUNDATION

IOWA METHODIST HEALTH SYSTEM